Food Hygiene

CORNWALL COLLEGE
LEARNING CENTRE

Susan Blanch

Hodder & Stoughton

A MEMBER OF THE HODDER HEADLINE GROUP

Orders: please contact Bookpoint Ltd, 130 Milton Park, Abingdon, Oxon OX14 4SB.
Telephone: (44) 01235 827720. Fax: (44) 01235 400454. Lines are open from 9.00–6.00,
Monday to Saturday, with a 24 hour message answering service.
You can also order through our website www.hodderheadline.co.uk

British Library Cataloguing in Publication Data
A catalogue record for this title is available from the British Library

ISBN 0 340 858079

First Published 2003

Impression number   10 9 8 7 6 5 4 3 2 1
Year   2007 2006 2005 2004 2003

Copyright ©Susan Blanch 2003

The source for the quotation on page v is BBC/Radio website. Reproduced with permission.

Photograph credits: Photo 1.1, 2.1, 3.1, 4.1, 4.2, 5.1 TOGRAFOX/RD Battersby; Photo 2.2 Science Photo
Library/Sinclair Stammers; Photo 2.3 NHPA/Stephen Dalton; Photo 2.4 Science Photo Library/Martin Dohrn;
Photo 3.2 Science Photo Library/Simon Fraser.

Cover photo appears courtesy of Eric Poppleton/CORBIS

Typeset by Dorchester Typesetting Group Ltd, Dorchester, Dorset
Printed in Great Britain for Hodder & Stoughton Educational,
a division of Hodder Headline Plc, 338 Euston Road, London NW1 3BH
by J.W. Arrowsmiths Ltd

Contents

Introduction

You are probably reading this text because your job, or the job you intend to do when you leave college, involves the handling of food. There are a wide variety of job roles that involve handling food. Food hygiene doesn't apply only to people who work with food all the time in kitchens, for example, of restaurants, schools, hospitals and offices. It is also important for people who handle food as a part of their job. This includes workers such as those in care homes or nursery workers. They may need to prepare or serve food sometimes for residents or children in their care. It also applies to those who handle fresh foods such as meats, fish or cheeses in shops.

Definition
Food: anything intended for human consumption or used as an ingredient in the preparation of food

What is food hygiene?

Food hygiene is about making sure that food is safe to eat. It's about people being able to buy food from a shop or café or restaurant, knowing it is safe. It's about people eating food at school or in a nursing home or hospital, knowing that they won't suffer any illness or injury from it. Food hygiene is about making sure that food is protected from the risk of contamination at every stage in its preparation until it is eaten.

Definition
Contamination: when unwanted items or bacteria are present in food

WHO IS RESPONSIBLE FOR FOOD HYGIENE?

Everyone who handles food during their work has some responsibility for food hygiene. All food handlers should be aware of how contamination of food can be prevented. Supervisors and managers in food businesses are also responsible for ensuring that their staff follow hygienic procedures for handling food.

WHY IS FOOD HYGIENE IMPORTANT?

Food hygiene is an important and topical issue. The UK Government is concerned with making sure that the food we eat is safe. Every year cases of food poisoning and food-related illness are reported in the news – *E. coli*, *Salmonella* and *Listeria* outbreaks are recent examples. Each time, the Government holds inquiries as to the causes. Recommendations are made about how outbreaks can be prevented in the future. All the outbreaks are caused by poor standards of food hygiene somewhere in the manufacture, storage, preparation or serving of food. The law now requires training in food hygiene for all food handlers. Managers and supervisors in food businesses are being encouraged to take action to protect their businesses and their customers. The Government is concerned with ensuring that food is properly handled from the time it leaves the field until the time it reaches the plate.

There are more than just legal reasons for the importance of food hygiene, though. If you are the chef or manager in a restaurant, it is good business sense to have high standards of food hygiene. You will lose customers very quickly if you develop a reputation for serving poor food. When customers complain about suffering the effects of food poisoning they won't complain just to you. In fact, they may not complain to you at all, but they will tell their friends. This may mean that your customers start to go somewhere else.

Britney's restaurant apologises ...

Britney Spears' new restaurant Nyla had to apologise to three diners who claim they got food poisoning after eating there. The three girls all complained of vomiting and diarrhoea after eating the wild striped bass. The New York restaurant, which only opened last week, is to give them gift certificates to say sorry.

(BBC Radio 1 News, 4 July 2002)

Food hygiene also makes sense from a cost point of view. If food becomes contaminated it has to be thrown away. So it makes sense to store, handle and use food properly so it doesn't have to be wasted.

What does this book do?

This book provides a comprehensive and practical approach to food hygiene. It will be of use to you as a student or a professional involved in food handling. You will find all the information you need about food hygiene along with exercises to help you practise and check what you have learned.

If you are taking an exam in food hygiene, you will find that the tests at the end of each chapter will help you prepare for this. There are two types of questions:

▮ multiple-choice questions where you choose one of the given answers
▮ short-answer questions where you need to write a short answer.

You might like to practise these under exam conditions.

Note for teachers

The text covers the complete syllabus for the basic (level 1) and intermediate (level 2) levels of training offered in food hygiene by the main examining bodies in this field as the Royal Institute of Public Health (RIPH) and the Chartered Institute of Environmental Health (CIEH).

The test questions offered at the end of each chapter will help students prepare for food hygiene examinations. Level 1 qualifications are usually examined by means of multiple-choice questions. Level 2 qualifications are normally assessed through a written exam. Examples of both types of questions for student practice are given at the end of each chapter.

Note that the multiple-choice questions provided reflect the knowledge and coverage for level 1 qualifications. Short-answer questions reflect the type of questions asked in level 2 examinations.

1 Food-related illness

The main problems arising from poor food hygiene are food-related illnesses. This chapter looks at food poisoning and food-borne disease. You will learn about:

- the difference between food poisoning and food-borne disease
- the causes of food-related illness
- the symptoms of food-related illness.

What is food-related illness?

Food-related illness includes food poisoning and food-borne disease. It is useful to start by looking at the difference between the two. Food poisoning is an illness caused by eating food that contains either harmful substances, or micro-organisms that are living and growing on the food. Food-borne disease is caused by micro-organisms that are carried by the food but do not necessarily need the food to grow and survive.

For someone to become ill through food poisoning, large numbers of the micro-organisms usually need to be present in the food. Food-borne disease can be caused by a small number of the micro-organisms.

Definition
Micro-organisms: very small life forms such as bacteria and viruses

Note that not all micro-organisms are harmful. Some can actually be helpful, such as those used in the making of yoghurt and cheese. Those that are harmful and can cause food-related illness are known as 'pathogenic' (see Chapter 2).

Definition
Pathogenic micro-organisms or pathogens: micro-organisms that cause illnesses

Food poisoning

How many times have you, or someone you know, said 'It must be something I ate.'? Most of us recognise the common symptoms of food poisoning. We might also know

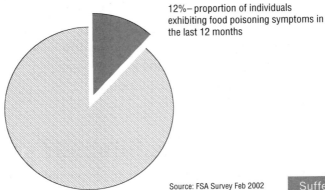 **Food Hygiene**

the sorts of food that are most likely to cause food poisoning. We are better educated than ever before about food poisoning, but it is still on the increase.

It is difficult to come up with accurate figures for food poisoning because most people don't report it. However, in February 2002, the Food Standards Agency published a survey which showed that five and a half million of us believed we had suffered from food poisoning in the last year (see Figure 1.1). That's about 12 per cent of the population. Of these, three-quarters believed that the cause was food prepared outside the home.

FIGURE 1.1

12% – proportion of individuals exhibiting food poisoning symptoms in the last 12 months

Source: FSA Survey Feb 2002

Sufferers of food poisoning

STUDENT ACTIVITY 1

Do a mini survey among the people you know. Ask them whether they have ever suffered from a food-related illness. Find out what symptoms they suffered, what they believe caused the illness and whether they saw a doctor. Try to ask at least five people.

You probably found that most people have suffered from a food-related illness at some time. Common symptoms are nausea, vomiting, abdominal pain and diarrhoea. Many will not have reported the incident to a doctor, which means that the real number of food poisoning cases is likely to be much higher than the reported numbers.

Why is food poisoning on the increase? There are lots of reasons that could cause this:

▮ We use a lot more 'ready meals' than we used to. Supermarkets sell a whole range of cooked foods that we reheat at home. As you will see later, reheating may give the micro-organisms time to grow.

▮ A lot more of us eat at restaurants regularly or buy take-away food. Because restaurants buy, prepare and serve lots of different foods, there are more risks for them to control than for someone cooking in their own kitchen.

▮ The amounts and different types of imported foods are increasing all the time. There may not be as many controls over the preparation and packaging of these foods in other countries as we have in the UK.

▮ Incorrect storage and cooking of foods at home can also cause food poisoning. We now have such a wide range of foods to use at home that means that we can sometimes get it wrong.

PHOTOGRAPH 1.1

Our eating habits have changed

Causes of food poisoning

Many people think that food poisoning is just caused by bacteria in food. Bacteria cause most cases of food poisoning but there are other causes as well. Food poisoning can be caused by any of the following:

■ pathogenic bacteria that are living on and growing in the food
■ moulds that produce toxins in the food
■ natural poisons that exist in the food
■ chemicals and metals that have been absorbed into the food.

Definition

Toxins: poisons produced by some bacteria and moulds

Bacterial food poisoning

Bacterial food poisoning can be divided into two groups:

■ Infectious food poisoning – this is where the illness is caused by eating large numbers of the bacteria. The bacteria then multiply in the intestines causing damage to the body tissues. You might have heard of *Salmonella*. *Salmonella* is a bacteria that causes this type of food poisoning.

■ Toxic food poisoning – this is where the illness is caused by toxins produced by the bacteria rather than by the bacteria itself.

Salmonella has been identified by the Food Standards Agency as the most common cause of food poisoning in England and Wales. Ninety per cent of reported cases of food poisoning are due to *Salmonella*. Here are just a few examples:

a 78 people suffered food poisoning symptoms following a wedding reception

b 36 people (including children) suffered illness after attending a primary school function

c 29 people (including 23 elderly people) suffered symptoms at a nursing home.

Salmonella was confirmed in each case.

(Information from Food Standards Agency Reports)

TOXINS

We have mentioned the toxins that bacteria sometimes produce. There are actually different types of toxins. They are classified according to when and where they are produced:

- Exotoxins are produced in the food as the bacteria grows and multiplies.
- Enterotoxins are released in the intestines as the bacteria multiply in the digestive system.
- Endotoxins are released in the stomach and intestines when the bacteria die.

FIGURE 1.2

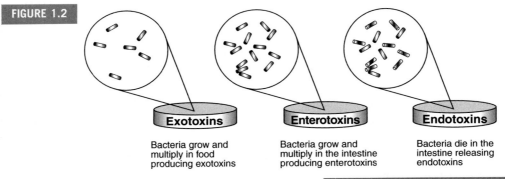

Exotoxins
Bacteria grow and multiply in food producing exotoxins

Enterotoxins
Bacteria grow and multiply in the intestine producing enterotoxins

Endotoxins
Bacteria die in the intestine releasing endotoxins

Bacteria can produce different types of toxins

SOURCES AND SYMPTOMS

Food poisoning sufferers will normally feel ill within a few hours, or at most a few days. Common symptoms of food poisoning include diarrhoea, nausea, vomiting and abdominal pain. The illness generally lasts a few days, though it can last longer.

You need to know about the more common food poisoning bacteria. Table 1.1 summarises the sources and symptoms of the most common food poisoning bacteria in the UK. It also gives incubation periods and the average length of the illness for each type.

Definition

Incubation period: the length of time normally taken for symptoms of the illness to appear

Table 1.1 Sources and symptoms of food poisoning bacteria

Bacteria	Sources	Symptoms	Incubation period	Average duration
Salmonella (infection)	Animals (rodents, terrapins, pets), raw meat, raw poultry, eggs, untreated milk, sewage and water	Vomiting, diarrhoea, abdominal pain, and fever. Can be severe for infants, elderly or infirm even leading to death. Sufferers can become carriers.	6–36 hours	1–7 days
Clostridium perfringens (toxin in the intestine)	Soil, dust, raw meat, animal and human faeces	Abdominal pain, diarrhoea and nausea though not usually actual vomiting. Usually a mild illness and deaths are rare.	8–18 hours	12–48 hours
Clostridium botulinum (toxin in food)	Soil, raw fish and meat, vegetables, tinned fish and corned beef	Breathing difficulties, difficulty in swallowing, slurred speech, dizziness, headache, muscle paralysis that can cause death. The organism produces a toxin that causes the symptoms.	12–36 hours	Several months
Staphylococcus aureus (toxin in food)	Human skin, nose, mouth and throat, infected cuts and boils, animal skin, raw cow or goat milk	Abdominal cramp, vomiting, low body temperature. Deaths are rare though the severity of the vomiting may require sufferers to be hospitalised. Toxins that develop in the contaminated food cause the symptoms.	2–6 hours	24–48 hours
Bacillus cereus (toxin in food or intestine)	Soil, dust, rice, other cereals and cereal products	Actually causes two different types of poisoning by producing two different toxins, one in the food and one in the digestive system: • food toxin causes nausea and vomiting • digestive system toxin causes colic and diarrhoea. Neither type of poisoning is likely to be fatal.	1–9 hours 8–16 hours	12–24 hours 24–48 hours

STUDENT ACTIVITY 2

Look at Table 1.1 and identify the micro-organisms that can cause:
▪ infectious food poisoning
▪ food poisoning caused by toxin in the food
▪ food poisoning caused by toxin in the intestines.
Make yourself a list of each type.

FIGURE 1.3

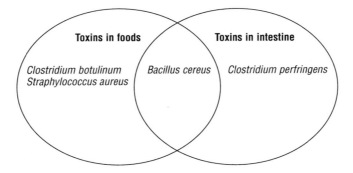

Toxins are produced in food by some bacteria and in the intestines by others

MOULDS

Moulds are micro-organisms that can cause spoilage in food. Most moulds are harmless and some are even used in food production such as in the making of blue cheeses.

Definition

Spoilage: the process of food becoming damaged. Spoilage bacteria will make food rot

A few moulds can cause illness by producing toxins in food. These toxins are known as 'mycotoxins'. The effect of mycotoxins is not fully understood. It is thought that some mycotoxins may be the cause of cancer in humans. One particular mycotoxin is thought to cause liver damage. There has been insufficient research on mycotoxins to establish a definite link.

Mycotoxins are thought to have been the cause of much illness throughout history. Toxins in wheat and grain can cause vomiting, convulsions and even gangrene in very serious cases. It is thought that many people may have died as a result of eating contaminated wheat. These sorts of health problems are now very rare. Our more varied modern diet prevents the build-up of mycotoxins. We also have a better understanding now of the importance of protecting foodstuffs from spoilage.

DID YOU KNOW?

Illness from mycotoxins is rare now in the UK because of the controls on foods likely to contain them. There are strict European rules on levels of mycotoxins in foods such as peanuts and dried fruits. There are also controls over animal foods because mycotoxins can contaminate cows' milk if the cows are fed contaminated food. Tests are carried out on imported foods and contaminated goods are destroyed.

NATURAL POISONS

You wouldn't expect any food establishment to serve poisonous dishes, but there are some foods that contain natural poisons. These can be removed in preparation or by cooking. If the foods are not properly prepared or cooked, they can cause illness.

Red kidney beans

One example is red kidney beans. These are poisonous when raw but quite safe if they are boiled for 10 minutes. Anyone who eats beans that have not been properly cooked may suffer illness. The symptoms are nausea, vomiting and diarrhoea, which occur between one and six hours after eating the beans.

Fish and seafood

There is a variety of fish and seafood that have toxic parts. These parts must be removed before eating the fish. Fish and seafood in this group include crabs and puffer fish. The nerve tissue of the crab – known as dead men's fingers – should be removed before consumption, as should the intestines of the puffer fish.

Other fish that are usually safe can occasionally cause illness. One group of fish, which includes tuna, mackerel and bonito, can contain high levels of histamine produced by bacteria in the fish. This is not always obvious from their appearance and smell. If the fish is eaten it can cause facial and neck rashes, diarrhoea, headache and difficulty in swallowing. The symptoms will appear within minutes of eating the fish. This is known as scombrotoxic poisoning.

Contaminated shellfish may cause paralytic shellfish poisoning (PSP) or diarrhitic shellfish poisoning (DSP). The shellfish – oysters, mussels or clams – become toxic after feeding on toxic plankton. This plankton only blooms at certain times of the year so the fishing season is restricted in waters where the plankton is known to grow.

PSP causes a tingling or burning sensation around the mouth, face and neck that spreads to the rest of the body. Symptoms will appear within 30 minutes of eating the contaminated shellfish. Death can occur within two to twelve hours where sufficient toxin is consumed. DSP causes nausea, vomiting, abdominal pain and chills that can start up to twelve hours after the shellfish was eaten.

The Government's Food Standard Agencies in England, Scotland and Wales constantly monitor coastal waters for shellfish poisons. They periodically ban fishing from some shellfishing areas where levels of the poisons are unacceptable. However, it is difficult to stop poachers and casual fishers who put themselves and others at risk.

Mushrooms

Some mushrooms such as wood blewits and morels are poisonous if eaten raw. They will cause nausea, sickness and abdominal pain if not properly cooked. These sorts of mushrooms were, in the past, only available in the wild. Now they are cultivated and can be bought for use in the home or catering businesses.

CHEMICALS AND METALS

Chemicals and heavy metals absorbed into food may lead to illness if consumed in large enough amounts. Chemical contamination is usually in the form of pesticides. Heavy metals are copper, lead, tin, aluminium and mercury.

Chemical poisoning

Crops can absorb pesticides during growth. The food might then be used in its natural state or used to produce food products for humans or animals. Either way, the pesticides find their way into human foods and can cause illness. Poisoning can occur also from consumption of fish caught in waters contaminated with chemicals.

Symptoms of chemical poisoning will vary depending on the type of poisoning and the amounts consumed. In many cases, it affects the nervous system. Where large amounts of the toxic substance are consumed, illness will occur quite quickly. In other cases, the effects may be cumulative. With some pesticides, for example, the poison builds up in the body over time and it can be difficult to ascertain the cause of illness.

In 1990, 50 children from a London school were taken to the local hospital emergency department suffering sudden nausea, sickness and abdominal pain. Tests showed that the most probable cause was cucumbers served at lunchtime that had been contaminated with Aldicarb.
Aldicarb is a pesticide used to control pests such as greenfly. Pesticides cause particular problems where they are sprayed on to crops just before harvesting and the food is not properly washed or peeled.

Chemicals are also added to foodstuffs as preservatives, colourings and flavourings for example. These will have been tested before use and don't generally cause health problems though they can set off allergic reactions. Sometimes the consumption of large amounts of a permitted food additive can cause illness. The most common of these is monosodium glutamate, which is used as an additive in many Chinese and other oriental foods.

There are more than 11 million chemical substances known to humans. Around 60 000 to 70 000 of these are in regular use. Around 600 new chemical substances enter the marketplace each month. Controlling all these substances gives governments around the world a difficult job.

(Information from Department of Health website)

Metals

Metal poisoning will cause vomiting and abdominal pain within an hour, if sufficient quantities are eaten. Toxic metals include antimony, cadmium, copper, lead, tin and mercury. Metals can contaminate food during growth or during processing. The following will give you an idea of how they can contaminate food:

- Antimony – used in the enamel coating of equipment and will not normally cause problems unless enamel is chipped.
- Cadmium – used to plate utensils and some parts of electric cookers and fridges. Can be attacked by acids in some foods and may then contaminate them.
- Copper – used in fittings for equipment such as drinks machines. Worn fittings may contaminate food. Copper can also cause fats and oils to turn rancid.
- Lead – lead from petrol can poison foods as they grow. Lead is also used in the glaze of some earthenware and can be released if in contact with acidic foods.
- Tin – if tinned foods are kept for too long, the acid in the food can begin to break down the metal and it may be absorbed into the food.
- Mercury – used in a variety of industries. Its accidental release into water or on to land may cause contamination of food.

In the 1950s and 1960s waste containing a mercury compound was released into the seas off Japan. It caused plankton to become contaminated, which then contaminated fish. Fifty-two people died from eating contaminated fish but hundreds of others subsequently developed symptoms that could be linked to the incident.

Chemical and metal poisoning are actually quite rare in the UK but the possibility shouldn't be overlooked.

Food-borne disease

Food-borne diseases are bacterial diseases that can be spread by contaminated food or water. Many, such as typhoid and cholera, are now rare in this country because we have clean drinking water and generally high standards of personal hygiene. We do however have outbreaks of some food-borne diseases. You may have seen news items relating to outbreaks of *E. coli*, which is a food-borne micro-organism causing disease.

In 1996 there was an outbreak of *E. coli* in Scotland. There were over 500 cases and 21 deaths. The outbreak was traced back to one butcher's shop. The food involved included cold cooked meats and cooked steak with gravy. As a result, the Government set up the Pennington Group. They investigated and made recommendations about how similar situations might be avoided in future. Among other things, they recommended that:

▌ There should be better food hygiene controls in butcher's shops.
▌ Raw and cooked meats should be separated.
▌ All food handlers should be trained.

Unlike bacterial food poisoning where, usually, large amounts of the bacteria need to be consumed, consuming very few organisms can cause food-borne disease.

Symptoms of food-borne disease can take much longer to appear, even months. Also, the illness may last for a few days or for years, causing long-term health problems. Symptoms vary but can be similar to those of food poisoning. Both food poisoning and food-borne illness can lead to death in severe cases.

Table 1.2 gives details of the main food-borne diseases.

STUDENT ACTIVITY 3

In each of the following cases, check the food poisoning and food-borne disease tables and explain which organism is most likely to be the cause of illness.

▌ Tony wakes in the night suffering from diarrhoea and vomiting, abdominal pain and fever. He had eaten roast chicken for tea, and suspects it was not cooked right through.
▌ Several people in a small Derbyshire town are affected by symptoms of diarrhoea containing blood, vomiting, abdominal pain and fever. All those affected bought and ate meat from the same butcher's shop.
▌ Mary is suffering from flu-like symptoms after attending a continental cheese and wine tasting.

People at risk

Anyone may become ill with food poisoning or food-borne disease if they eat contaminated food. In most cases it is not serious and the sufferer will recover within a few days. There are some groups of people, though, who may suffer more severe symptoms and even die from food-related illnesses. These include:

▌ very young children
▌ elderly people
▌ people who are ill or frail
▌ pregnant women and mothers who are breastfeeding.

These groups of people – or their carers – need to be particularly careful about food.

Table 1.2 Causes and symptoms of food-borne diseases

Illness	Bacteria/Cause	Sources	Symptoms	Incubation period
Typhoid and paratyphoid fevers	*Salmonella typhi* and *Salmonella paratyphi*	Human carriers are main source of disease through water or food contaminated by human faeces or handled by a carrier. Contaminated shellfish and insects may be a source of infection.	Headache, fatigue, fever, constipation, spots. Paratyphoid has similar but less severe symptoms. The illness may last several weeks and relapses are common. Can result in death.	1–3 weeks
Hepatitis A (infective jaundice)	Hepatitis virus	Contaminated shellfish and water supplies. Poor hygiene of a carrier. Carriers may not experience symptoms.	Anorexia, nausea, vomiting, fever, fatigue, abdominal pain, jaundice, swelling of liver. Can cause liver damage and sometimes death. Illness lasts several weeks and liver may take up to six months to recover. Children and young adults are most at risk.	7–40 days
Bovine tuberculosis	*Mycobacterium bovis*	Raw milk and dairy products from infected animals. Airborne transmission between humans.	Lung congestion, night sweats, wounds fail to heal, damage to body by the organisms. Sufferers can be affected for years.	4–6 weeks
Giardiaisis	*Giarda lamblia* (parasite)	Water contaminated by human faeces containing the cysts.	Cysts penetrate intestines causing discomfort, nausea, diarrhoea. Not very common. People can carry the disease without having symptoms.	5–25 days
Cryptosporidiosis	*Cryptosporidium* (parasite)	Water contaminated by infected human or animal faeces. Direct contact with infected animals.	Diarrhoea, vomiting, fever, abdominal pain	10 days
E. coli infection	*Escherichia coli*	Water, raw/undercooked meat, human and animal gut, sewage, untreated dairy products. Lives in the intestines of cattle and can contaminate meat.	Bloody diarrhoea, vomiting, abdominal pain, fever, kidney damage or failure. Old people and young children are particularly susceptible and may experience cramps and confusion.	12–24 hours
Dysentery	*Shigella sonnei*	Water, milk, salads, flies and cockroaches	Diarrhoea with or without blood, fever, abdominal pain, vomiting	1–7 days

Table 1.2 Causes and symptoms of food borne diseases – continued

Illness	Bacteria/Cause	Sources	Symptoms	Incubation period
Enteritis	*Campylobacter jejuni* (Note that there are many causes enteritis of which this is one)	Raw poultry, raw meat, milk, offal, animals	Abdominal pain, diarrhoea with or without blood, headache, fever, nausea	48–82 hours
Viral gastro-enteritis	Virus	Shellfish	Fever, abdominal pain, vomiting and diarrhoea	12–72 hours
Listeria infection	*Listeria monocytogenes*	Pâté, salads, soft cheeses, cheeses made with unpasteurised milk, chilled ready meals	Flu-like symptoms. In pregnant women can cause miscarriage or illness in the foetus. Can cause death.	7 days to several weeks

Chapter review

This chapter has given you an introduction to food-related illness. Food-related illness is a major concern for the Government and the general public. It is the main reason for food hygiene legislation. You have learned about the causes and symptoms of food poisoning and food-borne disease. You have also learned about the likely food sources of different types of food poisoning and food-borne disease. In the next chapter you will look at how micro-organisms grow in food and at other ways food can become contaminated.

Multiple-choice questions

1   Which of the following best describes 'food hygiene'?
   A   Keeping yourself clean as food handler
   B   Keeping the kitchen and equipment clean
   C   Keeping food clean at all stages during processing
   D   Keeping food safe at all stages of processing

2   Which of the following is the best definition of 'food poisoning'?
  A   Poisoning caused by chemicals or metals in the food
  B   Spoilage of food
  C   Illness caused by harmful substances or micro-organisms in the food
  D   Toxins in the food

3   Which is the best definition of 'contaminated food'?
  A   Food that contains anything that is harmful to health
  B   Food that contains micro-organisms that are harmful to health
  C   Food that has started to rot
  D   Food that has been touched by food handlers

4   Which of the following statements is true about micro-organisms in food?
  A   They are sometimes helpful
  B   They are never helpful
  C   They are always harmless
  D   They are always harmful

5   Which of the following best describes 'pathogenic micro-organisms'?
  A   Micro-organisms that live on food
  B   Micro-organisms that are used in the processing of food
  C   Micro-organisms that cause food to rot
  D   Micro-organisms that cause illness and disease

6   Which of the following describe the most common symptoms of food poisoning?
  A   Vomiting and cramp
  B   Abdominal pain, diarrhoea and vomiting
  C   Symptoms similar to flu
  D   Headache, blurred vision and vomiting

7   Which of the following is most likely to cause shellfish to become toxic?
  A   Pesticides
  B   Toxic plankton
  C   Natural poisons in the fish
  D   Chemical pollution

8　Which of the following types of food poisoning bacteria causes illness by producing a toxin in the intestines after being eaten?

　　A　*Salmonella*

　　B　*Clostridium botulinum*

　　C　*Clostridium perfringens*

　　D　*Staphylococcus aureus*

9　Which of the following best describes the symptoms of *Salmonella* infection?

　　A　Vomiting, diarrhoea, abdominal pain and fever

　　B　Breathing difficulties, slurred speech and headaches

　　C　Abdominal pain, vomiting and low body temperature

　　D　Abdominal pain, diarrhoea and nausea

10　Which of the following is most likely to be a source of *Salmonella*?

　　A　Shellfish

　　B　Corned beef

　　C　Peanuts

　　D　Eggs

Short-answer questions

1　Explain the terms 'food-related illness', 'food poisoning' and 'food-borne disease'.

2　Describe the main causes of food poisoning.

3　Identify three foods which may contain natural poisons and explain any procedures required to eliminate them.

4　Describe the principle symptoms and likely sources of the following illnesses: *Salmonella* infection, hepatitis A, *Clostridium botulinum* infection.

5　Explain the difference between infectious and toxic food poisoning.

2 Food hazards

Food hazards are anything that could contaminate food and make it unsafe to eat. In this chapter you will learn about:

■ how micro-organisms contaminate food
■ how you can recognise pest infestation and the hazards this may cause
■ physical and chemical contamination of food
■ how food becomes contaminated or cross-contaminated.

Definition
Hazard: anything that could potentially cause harm. Generally divided into biological, physical or chemical hazards

Microbiology

In Chapter 1 you learned about the illnesses that micro-organisms in food can cause. In this chapter, you will learn more about micro-organisms and how they contaminate food.

Micro-organisms are very small life forms. They are so small that they cannot be seen normally without using a microscope. Micro-organisms are everywhere. They are on and in our bodies. They are in the air we breathe. They are in water and soil. They are on animals and plants. Fortunately, most of these micro-organisms are harmless. You may remember that the ones that can cause illness are called 'pathogenic'. We are interested in the micro-organisms that can contaminate food. These include bacteria, viruses and microscopic fungi (moulds and yeasts).

Like any living organisms, micro-organisms need certain conditions in order to grow and survive. These include the following:

■ Food – all micro-organisms need some form of nutrition. All of the bacteria we are interested in and the moulds and yeasts require foodstuffs comprising sugars, protein, vitamins and minerals.

■ Water – few micro-organisms can survive without an available water supply.

■ Correct oxygen level – most micro-organisms require oxygen to grow. Some will only grow where there is no oxygen. This last group can grow in foods which have been canned, bottled or vacuum-packed.

■ Correct acidity/alkalinity level – levels of acidity are measured on the pH scale. The scale measures from 0 to 14, where 0 is the most acid, 7 is neutral and 14 is the most alkaline. Most micro-organisms prefer a pH that is around the neutral mark.

Food Hygiene

There are no bacteria that can grow in conditions where the pH is below 3.5. Moulds and yeasts are more tolerant and can grow in very acid conditions.

▊ Correct temperature – micro-organisms grow best in the temperature range between 5°C and 63°C. Some prefer colder temperatures than others. Outside this range, there are micro-organisms that can survive in very hot or very cold conditions but they will not grow and reproduce at these temperatures.

▊ Enough time – micro-organisms can reproduce quite quickly under ideal conditions. It may only take a few hours, for example, to develop dangerous levels of food poisoning bacteria in food.

▊ Lack of competition – if more than one type of micro-organism is present in a particular food, they will compete for nutrients. In favourable conditions, bacteria will grow fastest, followed by yeasts and then moulds. However, as the food spoils, the conditions may become less favourable for bacteria – more acidic, for example – and the other micro-organisms will take over.

| FIGURE 2.1 | **Inputs needed for growth** |

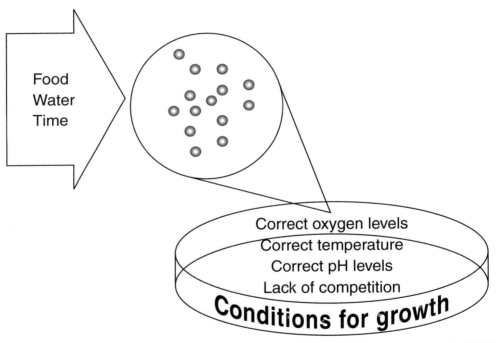

Food
Water
Time

Correct oxygen levels
Correct temperature
Correct pH levels
Lack of competition
Conditions for growth

The growth requirements for micro-organisms

STUDENT ACTIVITY 4

Look at the information above about the growth needs of micro-organisms. Which of the following foods do you think are most at risk from contamination by micro-organisms and which are least at risk? Explain the reasons for your answer in each case:

- raw meat left at room temperature
- pickled onions
- rice pudding left in a saucepan on the hob to cool down
- dried mushrooms.

BACTERIA

Bacteria are single-cell organisms. They multiply by splitting into two. Given ideal conditions, they can double their number every 20 minutes. This means that within a few hours, one organism can multiply to millions. It takes about one million organisms per gram of food to cause food poisoning.

FIGURE 2.2

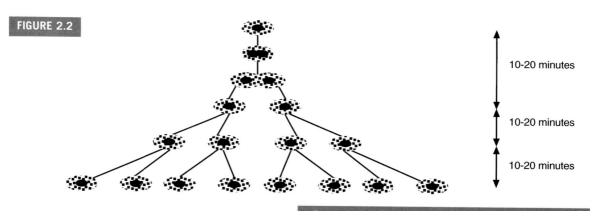

10-20 minutes

10-20 minutes

10-20 minutes

Bacteria multiply very quickly by splitting into two

Spores

Some types of bacteria can produce spores where the conditions for multiplication are unfavourable, for example where they run out of food, or where temperature or acidity levels change.

Definition

Spore: a hard, resistant body formed within the bacterial cell

When spores are formed within the bacterial cell, the remainder of the cell dies. The spore then remains dormant until conditions once again become favourable for growth. Spores can survive very unfavourable conditions for long periods of time. They are resistant to heat and cold so can survive cooking and freezing. They are also resistant to many of the chemical disinfectants used to kill bacteria.

Food Hygiene

There are two main types of bacteria found in food that form spores:

▮ bacilli
▮ *Clostridium*.

Bacteria come in different shapes. In fact they are classified according to shape:

▮ cocci are spherical, for example *Staphylococcus aureus*
▮ bacilli are rod shaped, for example *Salmonella*
▮ vibrio are curved rods, for example *Vibrio cholerae* which cause cholera
▮ spirochaetes are spiral shaped, for example *Leptospira* which are found in dirty water and can cause Weil's disease.

FIGURE 2.3

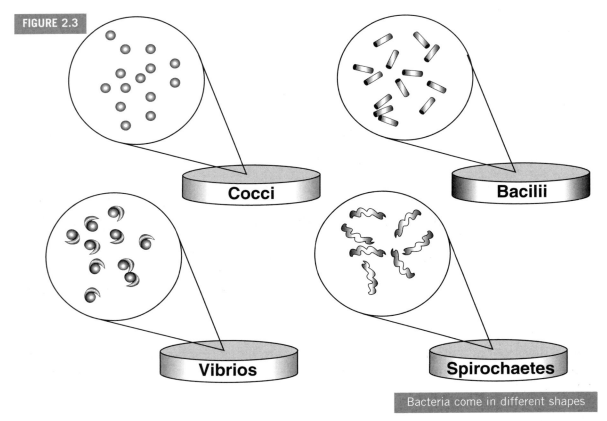

Cocci

Bacilii

Vibrios

Spirochaetes

Bacteria come in different shapes

VIRUSES

Viruses are the smallest micro-organisms. They cannot reproduce in food, but some can be carried by food. One example is hepatitis A virus. Viruses attach themselves to the living cells of a host organism and combine with them to produce further virus particles. The new particles attack further cells and the host will suffer disease. Viruses are always pathogenic. Host organisms can be humans, animals or plants.

Definition

Host organism: the person, animal or plant infected with the micro-organism

Most viruses are brought into food premises by food handlers who are carriers of the virus or by contaminated shellfish.

MOULDS

Moulds are multi-cellular organisms. They will grow on most foods whether they are dry or moist, high in sugars or salt, acid or alkaline. They can also grow in a wide range of temperatures. They grow fastest in humid conditions at temperatures between 20°C and 30°C.

Definition

Multi-cellular: consisting of more than one cell

Few moulds cause illness in humans but food affected by mould is generally considered to be unfit for consumption. Some moulds can produce mycotoxins that are dangerous to humans and animals (see Chapter 1).

Moulds reproduce by ripening and releasing spores into the air. Where these spores find a suitable food they will grow. Moulds commonly affect bread and other bakery products. They are difficult to avoid because – although cooking can destroy spores – they survive in the air and can contaminate food once it is cooked.

Some moulds are used in the production of food. For example, cheeses such as Roquefort, Danish blue and camembert are ripened by introducing moulds.

YEASTS

Yeasts are very simple, single-cell fungi. They reproduce by 'budding'. This is where part of the cell bulges out of the cell wall, grows and then separates to form a new cell. Yeasts break down the sugars and carbohydrates in food. Where there is no oxygen, the breakdown produces alcohol and carbon dioxide. Where oxygen is present, water and carbon dioxide are produced. The best growth temperature for yeasts is around 25°C and 30°C but they can grow in temperatures as high as 47°C and temperatures below 0°C.

FIGURE 2.4

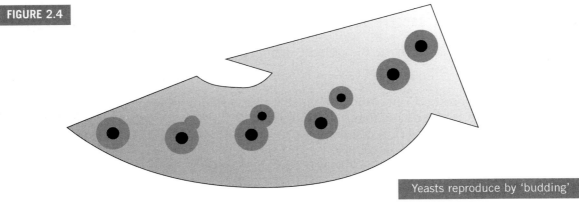

Yeasts reproduce by 'budding'

Yeasts are used in the production of vinegar and alcoholic drinks and in bread making. They can cause spoilage in foods such as fruit juices, jams, honey, meats and wines.

Spoilage

In Chapter 1 we looked at the different illnesses caused by micro-organisms in food and how this is the main hazard related to micro-organisms. However, anyone involved in the preparation of food should also be concerned with food spoilage. It is an offence to sell spoiled food, even though the spoilage organisms are not necessarily pathogenic.

Spoilage takes place in two different ways. The first is the natural decay process that starts when the food is harvested or slaughtered. Enzymes within the food start to break down the cellular structure and, if allowed to continue, will make the food unfit for consumption. The second method is where food is damaged or bruised and is then attacked by micro-organisms. These micro-organisms break down the food and may change its taste, smell and appearance. Bacteria, yeasts and moulds can all spoil food.

DID YOU KNOW? To some extent, the decision on whether food is spoiled or not depends upon the person who is preparing or eating it. For example, the Icelanders prepare a dish called 'hakarl' which is actually shark meat that has been buried for three months. Most people would consider it to be inedible but in Iceland it is a delicacy! A less extreme example is the British tradition of hanging game, such as pheasant and hare, to allow a stronger flavour to develop. In America, such meat would be discarded as spoiled.

In most cases, food spoilage will be obvious from the appearance, smell or taste of the food. Spoilage usually occurs as follows:

- Fruit is usually spoiled by moulds or yeasts which can grow in acidic conditions, after being damaged during storage or transportation.
- Vegetables can be spoiled by moulds or bacteria. Again, this is often as a result of damage during storage or transportation.

- Meat is broken down by enzymes in the meat, and can also be spoiled by bacteria.
- Fish is spoiled in a similar way to meat, though the process is usually much more rapid.
- Milk and milk products are usually spoiled by bacterial growth that causes the product to sour. These bacteria are present in the raw milk and survive processing. If left, moulds can also grow.
- Bread and other flour products are usually affected by moulds and yeasts because of the high sugar levels.
- Canned foods can spoil where bacteria have not been properly destroyed before canning, where the can is not properly sealed, and where the can itself is eroded by acids in the food.

PHOTOGRAPH 2.1

Mouldy food is generally considered unfit to eat

STUDENT ACTIVITY 5
Identify three foods that you have seen spoiled and describe the effects of spoilage on texture, taste and appearance.

Table 2.1 describes common signs of spoilage in different foods.

Table 2.1 Signs of spoilage in food

Type of food	Common signs of spoilage
Milk	Smells and tastes 'off'. Starts to curdle so bits are found in the milk
Vegetables	Become soft and discoloured. May have black spots. Smell rotten
Fish	Smells 'off' and discolours
Processed/cooked meats	Surface slime and discoloration. Smells 'off'. Produces gases that may burst vacuum packs
Fresh meats/poultry	Surface slime. Green discoloration. White spots. Smells 'off'
Bread	Fruity, sickly smell. Soft sticky texture. Internally bread discolours to yellow or brown

Micro-organism facts
- Most micro-organisms are harmless.
- Some micro-organisms are beneficial and used to produce food and drinks.
- Pathogens are micro-organisms that cause illness.
- Bacteria and moulds can cause illness and spoilage of food.
- Yeasts only cause spoilage of food.
- Viruses only cause illness.

Food pests

Another hazard in food premises is the presence of food pests. Food pests include rodents, insects or birds that cause damage to, or contamination of, food products. They are attracted by the presence of food and the warmth and shelter offered by food premises. Bodies or body parts, fur, eggs and droppings can all contaminate food. Pests can also carry pathogenic and spoilage bacteria and viruses that will contaminate the food. Note that raw foods may already be contaminated by food pests when they arrive at the premises. Any deliveries need to be checked on arrival and rejected if they are contaminated.

Table 2.2 (on pages 24–25) gives details of the most common food pests. It describes the hazards from each type of pest and the signs to look for when you suspect infestation.

Most of the food businesses that are closed down each year by Environmental Health Departments are closed due to the presence of food pests. Many complaints made to Environmental Health Departments about food businesses are to do with pests.

STUDENT ACTIVITY 6
What might the following signs indicate in food premises and what hazards might they present?
- dead, brown flat insects and egg cases around food storage areas
- gnawed wiring on equipment and woodwork, and droppings in food premises
- dead bluebottles around food preparation areas.

PHOTOGRAPHS 2.2, 2.3, 2.4

Pests are attracted to food premises

Table 2.2 Sign of food pests and related hazards

Pest	Characteristics	Hazards	Signs of infestation
Rodents			
Black rat	An agile animal with pointed nose, long tail and large ears. Also known as the ships' rat and tends to be confined to areas around ports. Prefers fruit and vegetables.	• All rodents can carry pathogenic and spoilage organisms which will contaminate foods • Droppings, urine, fur or dead bodies may be deposited in food • Damage to premises by gnawing woodwork, metal pipes, electric cables, etc	• Dropping and urine smears • Fur • Dead bodies • Sightings of live animals • Runways – worn tracks to feeding points • Footprints and tail marks • Damage to premises and equipment due to gnawing • Smell from nests
Brown rat	Larger and more common than the black rat with small ears and shorter tail. Also known as the Norway or common rat. Lives in sewers and drains, wall or floor cavities or in piles of rubbish. Prefers cereal foods.		
House mouse	Small with pointed head, large ears and a very long tail. They breed rapidly and will nibble food and non-food items. They prefer cereal foods.		
Flying insects			
Flies	Houseflies, bluebottles, greenbottles, and fruit flies are all of concern in food premises. They feed by regurgitating enzymes on to the food to break it down, then suck up the food. They feed on rubbish, and human and animal faeces as well as foodstuffs. They breed very rapidly in warm weather.	• Carry pathogens or spoilage bacteria on their bodies • Defecate on food as they eat • Regurgitate parts of previous meals which could be contaminated • Lay eggs in food • Maggots hatch, eat and pupate in the food • Adult flies may die in the food	• Live or dead insects in and around food • Maggots or pupae on food
Wasps	Wasps favour sweet foods and are particularly common around food premises in late summmer and early autumn.	• Can carry pathogens picked up from rubbish • Can cause panic among staff in busy food premises	• Live or dead insects in or around food
Crawling insects			
Ants	Food premises attract black ants (garden ants) and pharaoh's ants. Black ants will infest food premises in their search for sweet foods. Pharaoh's ants are smaller and pale yellow. They live in warm premises and, as well as sweet foods, will feed on high protein foodstuffs such as meat.	• Spread pathogenic organisms • Dead bodies may contaminate food	• Live or dead insects in or around food • Presence of nests in premises though these may be difficult to detect

Table 2.2 Signs of food pests and related hazards – continued

Pest	Characteristics	Hazards	Signs of infestation
Cock-roaches	Two types are found in the UK: the oriental cockroach and the German cockroach. The oriental cockroach is brown with a flat body and about 25 mm in length. They are often found in damp conditions. The German cockroach is about 15 mm in length, yellowish brown, with a flat body and prefers humid conditions. Neither species can fly and both feed on waste food.	• Carry pathogenic organisms including *Salmonella* • Egg cases, faecal pellets and bodies in food	• Live and dead insects • Faecal pellets • Egg cases or larvae • Odour
Silverfish	Fish-shaped, grey bodies with very long antennae. Live in damp conditions and often found under carpets or wallpaper.	• Don't contaminate food directly but can fall into food	• Live and sead insects
Stored product insects			
Psocids	Also known as book lice, they are very small and brown or cream in colour. Generally feed on moulds from walls, containers and food, though will eat foodstuffs such as flour. Breed quickly in warm, damp conditions.	• Not a direct health hazard but they can infest food particularly where it is poorly stored	• Live and dead insects • Poor storage conditions
Grain weevils	The most common of the weevils, they are generally found in stored grain on farms but will infest foods such as pasta and flour. Lay eggs in food and the pupae feed on it as they hatch.	• Not a direct health hazard, but can leave eggs, pupae and bodies in foodstuffs	• Live and dead insects
Birds			
Birds	Any birds that gain access to food premises are a pest. Most often they are pigeons and sparrows, but other birds can cause problems.	• Carry pathogenic bacteria including *Salmonella* • Leave contaminated droppings and feathers in food • Can contaminate water supplies, particularly where dead birds fall into water tanks	• Live and dead birds • Droppings • Nest sites • Feathers

Contamination

Food is said to be contaminated when it contains any unacceptable matter. This can be in the form of micro-organisms, poisons, or physical contaminants. Physical contaminants might include items such as pieces of glass or metal. Contamination is generally divided into three types:

- microbiological
- physical
- chemical.

FIGURE 2.5

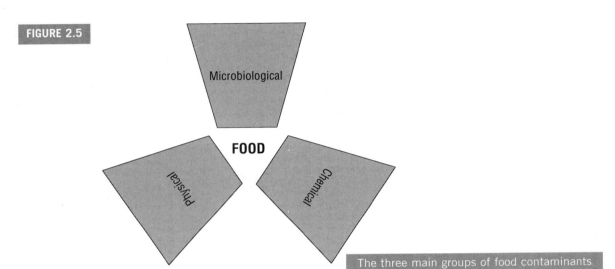

The three main groups of food contaminants

MICROBIOLOGICAL CONTAMINATION

FIGURE 2.6

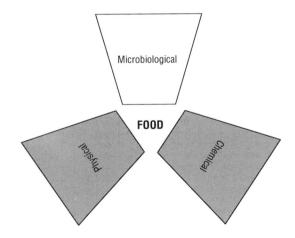

Much raw food does contain harmful micro-organisms, but these are generally destroyed or reduced to safe levels during preparation. It is contamination during and after preparation that often causes problems. This largely occurs as a result of:

- poor personal hygiene
- poor food handling
- inadequate food preparation
- poor storage areas
- presence of pests in food premises
- pets – can also carry pathogenic bacteria and should not be allowed in food premises.

Humans are probably the most common source of bacterial contamination of food. Inadequately washed hands, dirty clothes, and cuts and sores on hands can all be a risk to food safety. Some people may be carriers of a particular disease or virus, though they show no signs of illness, and may contaminate the food they handle. The risk from human sources is not just that from food handlers. Anyone who enters the food preparation area may be a source of bacterial contamination. People other than food handlers may be more of a risk as they will not be adequately dressed or prepared for handling food.

High-risk foods

There are some foods that are particularly attractive to microbiological growth. They tend to be foods that are moist and rich in protein. They include meat, fish, shellfish, poultry, eggs, milk and dairy products, cooked rice and pasta. Particular care is needed in handling these foods.

Definitions

High-risk foods: these include those that are high in protein and moist, such as meat, fish, shellfish, poultry, eggs, milk and dairy products, cooked

Times change! It used to be that babies and young children, elderly people and those who were ill were often given soft-boiled eggs. They were considered easy to digest and full of goodness. Since the scare about eggs and *Salmonella* in the late 1980s, the Government has recommended that none of these groups of people should be given raw or undercooked (including soft-boiled) eggs. Eggs are now considered to be one of the main sources of *Salmonella* and are classed as a high-risk food.

rice and pasta

Cross-contamination

Micro-organisms cannot move from one place to another on their own. Cross-contamination is where bacteria are transferred from one place to another on a vehicle. An example is where a knife or cutting board is used for raw meat and cooked meat. The organisms in the raw meat are transferred to the cooked meat on the knife and cutting board. The knife and cutting board act as vehicles for the micro-organisms.

Definition

Cross-contamination: when micro-organisms are moved from one place to another on a vehicle

Vehicle of contamination: any object (including persons and animals) on which micro-organisms can move from one place to another

Bacteria are transferred from their sources to prepared foods in a variety of ways:

▮ raw and cooked foods being stored together and touching

▮ drips and splashes from raw foods such as meat contaminating cooked foods

▮ air currents carrying organisms from raw food preparation areas

▮ kitchen equipment and utensils being used for raw and cooked foods without being properly cleaned

▮ raw and cooked foods being prepared on the same work surfaces

▮ cloths used for wiping equipment and surfaces

▮ bacteria carried on hands and clothing of food handlers

▮ food pests carrying bacteria from raw food and waste to cooked foods.

Of the people who attended a buffet at a Masonic lodge, 45 out of 55 became ill. Investigations showed that the likely source of contamination was the egg whites used to make meringue for a lemon meringue pie. The meringue was only lightly cooked so the organisms were likely to have survived the cooking process. It is also likely that there was cross-contamination because the bowl used to beat the raw eggs was then used to blend commercially bought mayonnaise and salad cream without being properly cleaned. This mayonnaise mixture was used to dress a number of salad dishes. These factors could account for the high rate of illness among the party.

PHYSICAL CONTAMINATION

FIGURE 2.7

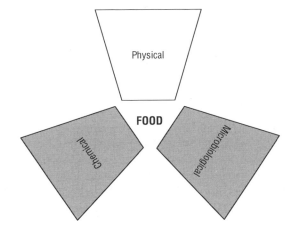

Physical hazards are any foreign objects that fall into the food at any stage during its production or preparation. There are a variety of sources of physical contamination:

- People – physical contamination from people may include things that fall into food from clothing such as buttons; things falling from pockets such as combs, money and pens; jewellery; cigarette ends; or matter from the person such as hair or fingernails. Plasters used to cover cuts on hands may also fall into food. Persons other than food handlers who enter the food preparation area may be more of a risk as they may not be adequately dressed or aware of the risks they present. These might include maintenance engineers and delivery people.
- Food – unwanted parts of food such as bones, pips, stalks can remain in the food after preparation.
- Packaging and containers – paper, glass, string, plastic and polythene from food packaging and damaged storage containers may contaminate food.
- Equipment and machinery – pieces of metal, glass, wood or plastic from damaged equipment or machinery can get into food as it is being prepared. Moulds or stale food from equipment that has been inadequately cleaned might also contaminate food.
- Premises – where premises are not adequately maintained, or where work being carried out is not properly separated from food preparation areas, there is a risk of contamination by bits of plaster or brick, flakes of paint, screws and nails, or broken glass. Where premises are not adequately cleaned, there is a risk of dirt and waste being transferred to food.
- Food pests – we have already mentioned the risks from food pests. Fur, feathers, bodies, faeces, eggs, or young of rodents, insects, and birds may all contaminate food.

CHEMICAL CONTAMINATION

FIGURE 2.8

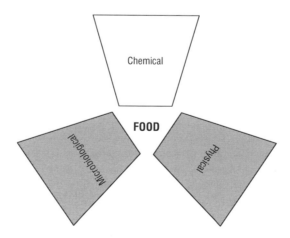

We mentioned two sources of chemical food poisoning in Chapter 1. Food can be poisoned by pesticides used during growing that have not been destroyed by the food preparation or chemical pollution in the environment.

There are also risks in food premises. Chemicals used in food premises may contaminate the food during storage or preparation. These include materials such as:

▌ cleaning materials

▌ lubricants or fuels for equipment and machinery

▌ substances such as fly sprays or pesticides.

These can contaminate food when they are not correctly stored and used.

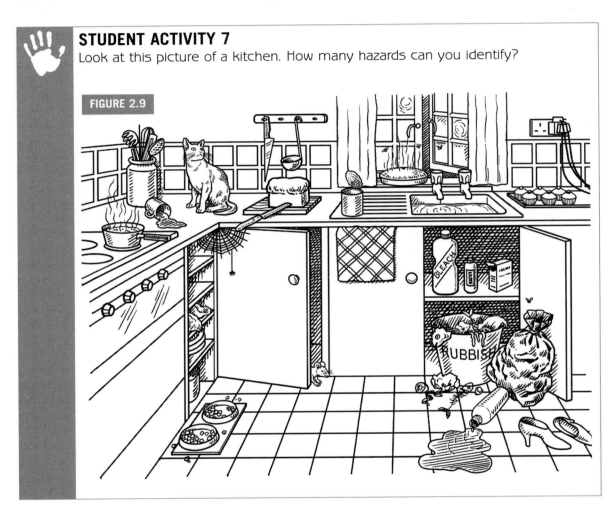

STUDENT ACTIVITY 7
Look at this picture of a kitchen. How many hazards can you identify?

FIGURE 2.9

Chapter review

In this chapter you have learned about microbiological, physical and chemical hazards to food. You have learned about food pests and how to recognise pest infestations. You have learned about how food can become contaminated and cross-contaminated. The next chapter looks at how these hazards can be controlled.

Multiple-choice questions

1 Which of the following best describes how bacteria multiply?

- **A** They grow buds which then separate off
- **B** They release spores into the atmosphere
- **C** Each cell splits into two
- **D** They lay eggs in the food

2 Which of the following best indicates the time taken for bacteria to multiply into millions of organisms?

- **A** A few minutes
- **B** A few hours
- **C** A few weeks
- **D** A few days

3 Which of the following reflects the temperatures at which bacteria are most likely to multiply?

- **A** Under 5°C
- **B** Between 5°C and 63°C
- **C** Above 63°C
- **D** Between zero and 70°C

4 Which of the following best describes a food pest?

- **A** Rodents
- **B** Birds
- **C** Insects and mites
- **D** All of the above

5 Which of the following is an example of a chemical contaminant?

- **A** Pathogens
- **B** Pesticides
- **C** Insect eggs
- **D** All of the above

6 Which of the following is true about moulds?

   A They are always pathogenic

   B They are always harmless

   C They are used in some food production

   D All food with mould should be discarded

7 Which of the following is true of bacterial spores?

   A They can survive in adverse conditions

   B They are the main way of reproducing

   C They cause food spoilage

   D They are produced by all pathogens

8 Which of the following is an example of a physical contaminant?

   A Pesticides

   B Pathogens

   C Insect eggs

   D All of the above

9 Which of the following is considered to be a high-risk food?

   A Bread

   B Eggs

   C Uncooked rice

   D Vegetables

10 Which of the following is most likely to be spoiled by yeast growth?

   A Jam

   B Beer

   C Vinegar

   D Bread

Short-answer questions

1 Explain how food becomes contaminated with micro-organisms.

2 Describe sources of chemical contamination.

3 Explain the effect of spoilage organisms on food.

4 What conditions are required for bacterial growth?

5 How do flies spread food poisoning and food-borne disease?

3 Control measures

This chapter looks at how food hazards can be controlled and reduced. You will learn about:

I how microbiological, physical and chemical hazards can be reduced and prevented

I how temperature control can be used to eliminate, reduce or prevent hazards and risks to food safety

I the different methods of food preservation and storage

I procedures for disposal of unsound foods

I how food pests can be discouraged or eliminated and the risks involved in chemical control methods.

Reducing and preventing contamination of food

In Chapter 2, we looked at the hazards that can exist in food premises and contaminate food. All food handlers are responsible, to some extent, for controlling or eliminating these food hazards to ensure that the food they prepare and serve is fit for human consumption. In this chapter we will look at how that reduction or elimination can be achieved. We will first consider some general methods of reducing risks before looking specifically at temperature control, storage and preservation of food, and control of food pests.

GENERAL CONTROLS FOR BACTERIAL RISKS

Precautions that can be taken to prevent bacterial contamination and cross-contamination include:

I Purchasing foods – especially high risk foods – from reputable suppliers. These companies should have good controls to prevent contamination.

I Good standards of personal hygiene, particularly with regard to hand washing. Hands should be washed after handling raw food, before handling cooked foods, after handling waste or visiting the toilet (see Chapter 4).

PHOTOGRAPH 3.1

Food purchases should be made from reputable suppliers

DID YOU KNOW?

Almost all bacteria can be removed from the hands by washing thoroughly with soap and water. Handwashing is, therefore, very important in the reduction of microbiological contamination.

- Minimising food handling wherever possible and using disposable gloves or clean utensils to handle, where appropriate. This will reduce the risk of bacteria being transferred from hands or utensils to food.

- Keeping raw and cooked foods apart in storage areas and food preparation areas. Raw foods are more likely to be contaminated but can cross-contaminate cooked foods if they are not separated.

- Using separate equipment and utensils for raw and cooked foods or thorough cleaning between uses. This avoids cross-contamination between raw and cooked foods.

- Making sure equipment, utensils and surfaces are properly cleaned between uses. Bacteria may survive on equipment, utensils and surfaces especially if they are dirty.

- Proper disposal of empty food containers that may contain spoiled or contaminated waste. Spoiled or waste scraps of food on empty containers could contaminate other foods.

- Keeping displayed and stored foods properly covered. This prevents contamination by airborne micro-organisms.
- Keeping food areas free from waste. Bacteria will build up in waste and can then contaminate foods being prepared or served.
- Preventing staff with health problems from handling food – this includes anyone suffering from diarrhoea and sickness, anyone with severe nose and throat infections or coughs, anyone with skin disease or infected cuts or boils. Pathogens can easily be transferred to food from infected persons.

GENERAL CONTROLS FOR CHEMICAL RISKS

When it is necessary to keep chemicals on food premises, they should be properly stored in their appropriate containers. They should be kept in locked cupboards away from food storage and preparation areas, used in accordance with given instructions, and disposed of carefully and safely after use.

GENERAL CONTROLS FOR PHYSICAL RISKS

Food handlers need to take precautions to ensure that they do not contaminate food with any foreign bodies. These precautions include the wearing of appropriate clothing, including hair coverings, not wearing jewellery and not carrying objects in pockets which could fall into food. Managers can reduce risks by ensuring the proper maintenance of premises and equipment, preventing smoking in food preparation areas, and controlling the entry of non-food handlers to food preparation and storage areas.

In larger food premises, such as food-processing plants, the use of metal detectors may help to eliminate some contaminants. Filters and sieves may help to remove some contaminants. The prevention of many physical hazards in food depends on the vigilance of the food-handling staff who should be properly trained to deal with these problems.

STUDENT ACTIVITY 8

Imagine you were asked to start work in the kitchens at your college or workplace in half an hour. List the preparations you would need to carry out in order to avoid or reduce risks of physical contamination of food.

TEMPERATURE CONTROLS

The most effective way of controlling the growth of micro-organisms in food is by the use of temperature. We saw in the last chapter that micro-organisms thrive at temperatures between 5°C and 63°C. Foods, especially high-risk foods, should be kept out of this danger zone as much as possible. Risks arise where foods are:

- left at room temperature
- left in sunlight, such as in a shop window
- heated or cooled slowly.

Micro-organisms can be destroyed by heating food. It is important that foods are cooked and heated using appropriate methods and temperatures.

FIGURE 3.1

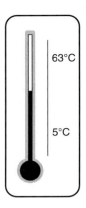

63°C

**Microbiological growth:
the danger zone**

5°C

Food should be kept out of the 'danger zone'

The rules for heating and cooling foods

▮ Liquids should be cooked in amounts small enough to ensure even temperatures throughout, and stirred frequently.

▮ Re-heating of cooked foods is best done quickly in infrared units, microwave ovens or forced air-circulation ovens.

▮ Food should be cooked or reheated to at least 75 °C to destroy any organisms. This should destroy most organisms but spores may survive.

▮ If food is to be eaten cold, it should be cooled quickly to prevent new bacterial growth.

The best way to cool food is in a blast chiller or a separate refrigerator specifically used for cooling. It should never be placed in a refrigerator, freezer or chiller cabinet with other foods as it may raise the temperature of the refrigerator and of other foods allowing bacteria to grow. It can also cause condensation that would increase the risk of cross-contamination.

Using frozen foods

There are also risks when thawing frozen foods.

▮ It is important to ensure that food is completely thawed before cooking. Sufficient time must be allowed for this. If the centre of the food is still frozen when cooking is begun, it will warm up slowly and provide an ideal breeding ground for bacteria. This is particularly dangerous with foods such as poultry that can carry *Salmonella*.

▮ Food that is being thawed should be kept separate from other foods as the liquid from the item being thawed can contaminate other foods. Thawing should ideally take place in a thawing cabinet or room, or refrigerator set aside for the purpose.

▮ Microwave ovens can be used to thaw some foods.

▮ Food should not be re-frozen once thawed.

Table 3.1 summarises the temperatures and methods of storage and preparation of foods that should minimise the microbiological risks.

Table 3.1 Temperature controls for food

Chilling	These must be stored at a temperature below 8°C and it is safer to store them at a temperature below 5°C. Opening doors on chill cabinets or fridges will raise the temperature so must be kept to a minimum. Hot foods should not be put into chill cabinets with chilled foods, as this will also raise the temperature.
Freezing	Frozen foods must be stored at a temperature of −18°C or below. Again, opening freezer doors should be kept to a minimum as this will raise the temperature and hot foods should not be put into the freezers as this may cause frozen foods to defrost.
Thawing	Food should be placed in cold conditions to thaw (usually between 10°C and 15°C) not allowed to thaw at room temperature. It must be completely thawed before cooking.
Cooling	Where foods are to be served cold or cooled for later reheating, they must be cooled as rapidly as possible. They should then be stored at temperatures below 8°C.
Hot holding	If food needs to be kept hot (for example on a carvery or hot buffet), it should be held at 63°C or above. Food should be kept hot for the minimum amount of time.

DID YOU KNOW There are government regulations about temperature control of food which say that no person should keep food products that are at risk from pathogenic micro-organisms or toxins at temperatures that might result in a risk to health. Food here includes raw materials, ingredients, intermediate products or finished products.

(The Food Safety (Temperature Control) Regulations 1995)

FIGURE 3.2

There are regulations about food storage temperatures

CHECKING TEMPERATURES

Checks should be carried out to make sure all foods are being stored at the right temperature. Temperatures should be checked using appropriate measuring equipment. Records should be kept of the readings.

There are all sorts of equipment available for checking temperatures. Any equipment such as freezers, chill cabinets, etc. should show temperatures but they only show a general reading for the equipment. The food temperature should also be checked. Measuring the surface temperature of foods will not always give an accurate picture as food won't necessarily be at the same temperature all the way through. If there is any concern that food is not at the right temperature, then further checks must be done.

Probe thermometers can be used to check the temperature at the centre of food. A sharp probe attached to a thermometer is pushed into the food. The problem with probe thermometers is that they need careful washing between checks to avoid cross-contamination, and some foods will not be useable after testing. For example, testing foods that are sealed, such as vacuum-packed fish or cartons of yoghurt, will puncture the packaging – making the food unsaleable.

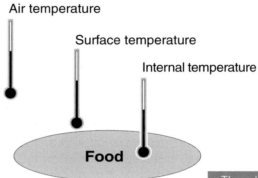

FIGURE 3.3

Air temperature

Surface temperature

Internal temperature

Food

Three levels of temperature testing

DID YOU KNOW ?

Infrared thermometers are now widely used for checking food temperatures. These can scan foods rapidly and identify any problems. For example, if you had a large delivery of frozen foods, traditional temperature-checking equipment would involve carrying out several checks on different boxes to ensure they were all at the appropriate temperature. With an infrared thermometer the whole order can be scanned quickly and the equipment will pick up any hotspots that need to be checked further.

When to check temperature

The number of temperature checks carried out will depend on the process or storage method:

■ Throughout the day, food on display – either hot or cold – should be checked frequently.

■ Daily checks should be carried out on refrigerators, refrigerated display cabinets and freezers.

■ Other checks should be carried out as required. These include checks on food that is delivered, food that is thawed, food that is cooked, food that is reheated, food that is cooled.

You will learn more about the importance of temperature in storage and preservation of food later in this chapter.

STUDENT ACTIVITY 9
Explain the risks in each of the following cases and describe how you would ensure food safety:
■ thawing a frozen chicken
■ cooking a previously frozen chicken
■ storing seafood
■ serving food from a hot holding area.

FOOD STORAGE

The proper storage of foods is essential to ensure good food hygiene. If food is not stored correctly, there is risk of contamination and spoilage. As well as being a risk to health, this can also lead to unnecessary wastage of foods.

Dry food stores

Dry foods include pasta, rice, dried fruits, dried milk, flour and cereals, and canned foods. The storage area needs to be dry, cool and well ventilated. Internal surfaces should be well finished so that they are easy to clean. The store should restrict any access by pests. If the area is well-lit, this will allow users to properly check for any deterioration or damage to food. Storage of food should be on open shelving which is raised from the floor. Cupboards with doors can provide hiding places for food pests and so should not be used.

Flours and cereals should be stored in lidded bins rather than their original sacks which can allow access by pests. These bins should be regularly cleaned and checked for signs of pest infestation. Canned foods should be regularly checked to identify damaged, dented or rusty cans. Other boxed foods will need checking for signs of deterioration, damage or infestation. Any spillage of food should be cleared up immediately to avoid attracting pests.

Stock rotation is particularly important. A 'First In, First Out' (FIFO) system should be adopted. Foods that were bought first, should be used first and all foods should be used or discarded by their use by/best before date. For items such as flour that are stored in containers, new stock must not be added to older stock in a container. The container should be emptied and cleaned before being re-filled with the new stock. Stores should be organised so as to prevent old stock being lost at the back of shelves.

Definition
FIFO stock rotation: first in, first out. Foods that were obtained first should be used first

Fruit and vegetable stores

Salads, fruit and vegetables need to be kept in cool, well-ventilated areas away from other foods. Many of these foods are purchased daily and stored for short periods. Root vegetables may be stored for longer periods. Fruit and vegetables should be stored in their boxes or containers. This reduces handling that can damage the food. The boxes should be stored on stainless steel shelving.

Boxes should be inspected on receipt for spoiled items that might damage the remaining fruits or vegetables. Checks should also be carried out for any pests that may have been delivered with the food. Salad and fruits which are served without being cooked or peeled can be sanitised in a very weak chlorine solution to destroy any micro-organisms.

Refrigerated stores

Refrigerated stores include refrigerators, freezers, walk-in chill stores and chill cabinets. They should be used to store high-risk foods – those most prone to bacterial contamination and spoilage.

Refrigerators and chill stores are used for storing perishable foods such as meat and dairy products for short periods. They should be set to operate at temperatures between 0 °C and 4 °C. Their temperature should be checked daily. This will minimise the risks of bacterial growth.

DID YOU KNOW ?

Some bacteria, such as *Listeria monocytogenes*, are able to grow slowly at low temperatures so chilling food will not stop growth. Provided the storage period is short, this should not be a problem because growth will be slowed down.

Refrigerators should be sited away from direct sunlight, and from any other source of heat. Motors should be readily accessible, regularly cleaned and well ventilated. Chill stores should be fitted with self-closing doors and plastic strip doors so the correct temperature can be properly maintained. It is important to keep refrigerators and chill stores clean, inside and out. Door seals should receive particular attention in order to prevent the build-up of dirt and damage.

Foods should be stored in refrigerators so that air can freely circulate. There should be enough refrigerated storage to deal with maximum demand and where possible there should be separate refrigerators for raw and cooked foods. Where this is not possible, foods should be stored as follows:

▌ top shelves – butter, lard, margarine, cheeses, eggs, convenience foods, cooked items, preserves, salad dressings, spreads and sauces

▌ centre shelves – cooked meats, milk products

▌ bottom shelves – raw meats, poultry and fish (this minimises the risk of cross-contamination by juices dripping on other foods)

▌ salad drawer – salad

▌ door racks – milk and fruit juices.

It is a good idea to label shelves according to use. If a shelf previously used for raw foods is to be used for cooked foods, it should first be disinfected. All foods should be stored in clean, labelled, covered containers. Canned foods should never be stored in open cans but should be transferred to appropriate containers. As with dry foods, stock rotation is important. All foods should be used or discarded by their use by/best before date. Foods obtained first should be used first.

STUDENT ACTIVITY 10
Look at this picture of a fridge and identify the hazards.

FIGURE 3.4

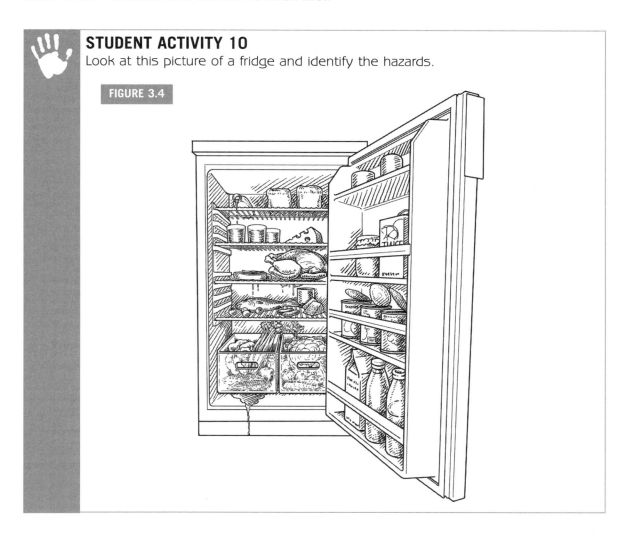

Freezers
Freezers should operate at around −18 °C or lower. Foods should be wrapped and can be tightly packed into freezers as this will prevent warm air entering when the freezer is opened. Freezers are generally designed to store ready-frozen foods. If they are to be used to freeze fresh foods, check the manufacturer's instructions about use. When frozen foods are delivered, the temperature should be checked. Any foods above −15 °C should be rejected.

Freezers should be fitted with an automatic temperature device and preferably an alarm. It is wise to keep the telephone number of the maintenance company to hand in

case of emergencies. All staff should be aware of procedures to be followed if freezers break down. If this happens, the freezer should not be opened and should be covered with newspapers or thick blankets as insulation. This will help to maintain the temperature. Food that has partially or fully thawed should never be re-frozen, though some items may be frozen again after cooking.

DID YOU KNOW ?

Ice-cream products are stored at higher temperatures than other frozen foods (generally between −7 °C and −4 °C). This is because they are eaten frozen and normal freezer temperatures would cause damage to the mouth and tongue. The law states, though, that they should never be stored above −2 °C.

Chill cabinets

Chill cabinets are refrigerated display units used in shops to display foods for sale. The food is cooled by cold air being circulated over the food. Draughts, sunlight and lighting in the cabinet can all affect food temperature and need careful control. Many need to be fully loaded to operate efficiently. The highest temperature allowed by Department of Health (DoH) regulations is 8 °C but a lower temperature should be used if it is thought necessary for the foods being stored. Different foods will require different temperatures. For example:

- ▮ milk needs to be stored at below 6 °C
- ▮ red meat at 7 °C
- ▮ red meat offal at 3 °C
- ▮ poultry at 4 °C.

FIGURE 3.5

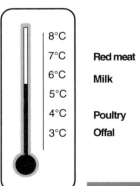

8°C	
7°C	Red meat
6°C	Milk
5°C	
4°C	Poultry
3°C	Offal

Different foods need to be stored at different temperatures

Hot holding

Hot cupboards are used to hold foods prior to serving. They are for foods that are already hot, not for re-heating food. Cabinets and containers should be heated prior to use to ensure food is not inadvertently cooled. Foods should be held for the minimum amount of time and must be kept at a temperature of at least 63 °C. The temperature should be checked frequently.

Delivery of food

Managers need to ensure that delivery areas are kept clean and free from pests to reduce the risk of contamination. Food should be transferred to proper storage areas as soon as possible after delivery. All foods should be checked before being moved to storage areas. Checking should cover:

- ensuring the correct foods have been received
- sell by/use by/best before dates
- checking for damage to packaging or food
- looking for any signs of pest infestation
- checking that foods – particularly frozen and chilled foods – are supplied at the right temperature.

STORAGE OF NON-FOOD ITEMS ON FOOD PREMISES

The storage of non-food items on food premises is unavoidable. These include cleaning and maintenance materials, personal items belonging to employees, and waste from food production and preparation. All of these are hazards in food-handling areas and need to be properly stored.

Cleaning and maintenance materials

Cleaning and maintenance materials can taint and poison food if allowed to contaminate it. All chemicals used in food-handling areas should be stored in suitable containers. These will usually be the ones in which they are supplied. They should be clearly labelled and securely stored away from the food-handling areas. All materials and equipment used for cleaning and maintenance should be locked away when not in use. Care should also be taken not to store together any chemicals which could react if mixed. The control of such items should be the responsibility of a designated staff member.

Personal items

Personal items include outdoor clothing, money, jewellery, handbags, etc. which might present micro-biological or physical hazards in food-preparation areas. Any food-handling establishment should provide storage facilities (usually lockers) in which staff members can store personal items. Clothing to be worn in food-handling areas will normally be stored close to the entry to those areas. Dirty clothing should be stored separately until it is sent to be laundered.

Waste

Waste in food-preparation areas can present microbiological and physical hazards if not properly stored. Suitable waste bins with tight fitting lids should be provided inside and outside food premises. Inside waste bins should be emptied several times during the day and always at the end of the day. They should be thoroughly cleaned before being re-used.

External waste-storage areas need to be kept clean and tidy to prevent infestation by pests. Surfaces should be regularly hosed down and waste bins washed out.

STUDENT ACTIVITY 11

Explain how you would ensure safe storage of the following items and list the risks of not storing them properly:

▌ raw meat
▌ flour
▌ canned foods
▌ cleaning materials.

FOOD PRESERVATION

We have seen that the growth of micro-organisms in food can cause changes to texture, smell, appearance and taste, as well as being a cause of illness in anyone who consumes the food. Preserving food extends its shelf life by limiting the growth of micro-organisms. There are many different methods of preserving foods. There are no methods which can preserve foods indefinitely. At some point, food will start to break down, micro-organisms will start to grow, or the packaging container may start to deteriorate.

In order to ensure people are informed about safe periods to keep foods, the Food Labelling Directive and Regulations require labels on pre-packed foods to show 'use by' or 'best before' dates. 'Best before' dates are used on foods that may become stale if kept for too long, but that don't present a problem with regard to the growth of dangerous micro-organisms. 'Use by' dates are required on foods that, if kept too long, may present a health risk if consumed. These are perishable foods which are at risk from the growth of dangerous micro-organisms.

While it is useful to be able to prolong the shelf life of foods, the method of preservation often changes the taste, texture or nutritional value of the food. In some cases this is quite acceptable. For example, pickled foods and fruit jams are popular in this state. Other foods will be acceptable to some people only as a matter of necessity. 'Long-life' milk has a different taste to fresh pasteurised milk, and lower nutritional value due to the treatment process. It may only be acceptable where there are no refrigeration facilities, or access to a milk supplier is very difficult.

STUDENT ACTIVITY 12

Make a list of at least five preserved foods that you eat and find acceptable even though the taste or texture is different from that of fresh produce. Are there any preserved foods you would not eat because the texture or taste has been changed by the preservation method?

If you compare your list to someone else's, you will probably find that there are differences. It's all a matter of personal taste! You might also find that you have identified a number of the preservation methods that we will look at here. Most of us buy at least some preserved foods, and many people today eat more preserved foods than fresh ones.

STUDENT ACTIVITY 13
List all the methods of preserving foods that you know.
Check your list against the preservation methods described below. Are there any you didn't include in your list?

Do you remember the list of requirements that pathogens and spoilage micro-organisms need to grow? Water, oxygen, correct pH levels, etc. Many methods of food preservation work by eliminating one or more of these so that the micro-organisms cannot survive.

FIGURE 3.6 **Inputs needed for growth**

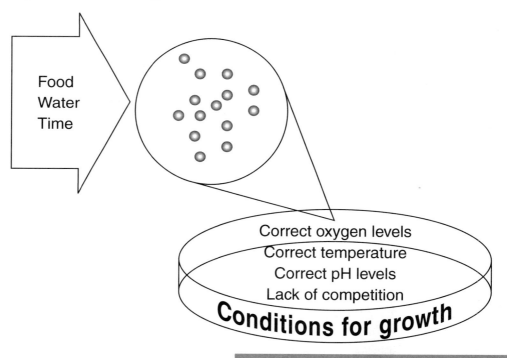

Food
Water
Time

Correct oxygen levels
Correct temperature
Correct pH levels
Lack of competition
Conditions for growth

The growth requirements for micro-organisms

Removing or reducing moisture
In Chapter 2, we discovered that micro-organisms need moisture in order to grow and multiply. By reducing the moisture in food, it is possible to make conditions intolerable for micro-organisms. This can give items a longer shelf life.

Food Hygiene

Drying has been used as a method of preserving food for hundreds of years. Traditional methods of drying include sun drying. This is still used today for foods like tomatoes and fruits. Some sausages and salamis are also allowed to air dry and, on some, specific moulds are encouraged because they help reduce the moisture content further.

Modern methods of drying include the following.

- Tunnel drying – food is placed on a conveyor belt and moves through a warm air tunnel. This is used for vegetables.
- Fluidised bed drying – warm air is blown up through the food particles and they are kept moving. This method is also often used for vegetables.
- Roller drying – food is applied to a heated roller as a thin paste. As the roller rotates, the food dries and is then removed from the roller by scraping. Usually used for potatoes and breakfast cereals.
- Spray drying – food in liquid form is sprayed into a drying chamber. As the spray mixes with warm air, the moisture evaporates leaving a powder residue. This is used to dry milk and eggs.
- Freeze drying – food is frozen, then heated in a vacuum. This causes the ice crystals to evaporate without first becoming liquid. The final product is porous so can be easily reconstituted in water. The method causes less change to the appearance, taste and nutritional value of the food than other drying methods. This method is used for a wide variety of foods including coffee, herbs, vegetables, shellfish and meats.

Lowering the pH value

While there are a few yeasts and moulds that can grow in very acidic conditions, most micro-organisms cannot tolerate a pH outside the neutral range (6 to 7). The addition of acid to the food, or of acid-producing organisms, will lower the pH value and limit the growth of dangerous micro-organisms. Both are traditional methods of food preservation.

FIGURE 3.7

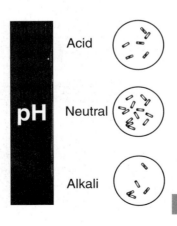

Micro-organisms usually only grow in the neutral range

■ Pickling – the addition of vinegar (acetic acid), has been long used as a method of preserving foods such as vegetables and fish.

■ Natural acids – fruit drinks such as orange juice contain citric acid and other natural acids that serve as preservatives.

■ Carbonising – fizzy drinks are protected by carbonic acid that is produced when the carbon dioxide is added to the drink.

■ Acid-producing organisms – a culture of specific, harmless micro-organisms is added to the food and produce acid that flavours and preserves the food. Yoghurt and sauerkraut (a German cabbage dish) are two examples of foods that are prepared using the addition of acid-producing organisms.

Smoking

Another traditional method of preserving food is smoking. As with some other traditional methods, smoking has been modified to meet modern tastes. Foods preserved in this way include fish, meat, poultry and cheese. The food is treated with brine or vinegar and then smoked over smouldering wood. The woods used are usually oak or ash and they must be free from any chemical preservatives. The smoke contains substances which inhibit the growth of spoilage bacteria. There are two different smoking processes:

■ hot smoking – used to cook foods as they are smoked. Used for fish and some cooked smoked meat

■ cold smoking – used for foods that will be cooked before eating such as smoked haddock.

PHOTOGRAPH 3.2

Smoking haddock

Food Hygiene

Traditional smoking gave a very strong flavour and modern smoking is a much less intense procedure that gives a better flavour but loses some of the preservative value. Modern smoked products should still be refrigerated, particularly when they have been vacuum packed.

Treating with chemicals

Natural and artificial chemicals are both added to food as preservatives.

Traditional methods using natural substances are:

- Curing or brining – meat and fish are cured by mixing dry salt with the raw food, soaking the food in brine, or injecting the brine into the meat through hollow needles. The salt limits the growth of micro-organisms. Some products such as bacon and herring are smoked in addition to curing. Producers today use less salt than was traditionally used by this method because current health concerns suggest that too much salt in the diet is not good for us. However, reducing the amount of salt used increases the risk of bacterial growth. It is important that food producers strike the right balance.

- Preserving with sugar – jams and crystallised fruits are two products that use sugar as a preservative. A large amount of sugar is required in order to preserve the food and prevent bacterial growth.

- Addition of spices or herbs – the essential oils in some spices and herbs have the effect of limiting bacterial growth when used in high concentration. Substances commonly used include cloves, cinnamon, mustard, onion and garlic. As with the use of salt, modern taste limits the use of these substances. Herbs and spices can themselves be a source of contamination where they have not been dried in hygienic conditions.

 **DID YOU KNOW?** The addition of salt or sugar to foods has a dehydrating effect. It reduces the moisture that would be available to micro-organisms. In effect, it binds the water molecules to the food making them unavailable to micro-organisms. Adding salt or sugars to foods are ancient methods of preservation which are still used today.

The use of artificial chemical preservatives is controlled under government regulations. There are 35 permitted preservatives in the UK. Each one is identified by an 'E-number'. Table 3.2 shows the more common preservatives and gives an indication of the wide variety of foods to which they are added.

Table 3.2 Food preservatives

Preservative	Examples of foods in which preservative is used
E200 sorbic acid	Yoghurts, sweets, soft drinks, processed cheese
E201 sodium sorbate	Frozen pizza
E202 potassium sorbate	Margarine, cheese spreads, salad dressings, glacé cherries, pre-packed cakes
E210 benzoic acid	Jams, beer, fruit juice, pickles, yoghurt
E211 sodium benzoate	Prawns, margarine, soft drinks, barbecue sauce, orange squash
E220 sulphur dioxide	Dried fruits, packet soups, fruit juices and syrups, dried vegetables, beer, wine, cider, sausage meat
E249 potassium nitrate	Cooked meats, sausages
E250 sodium nitrate	Cured meat, pork sausage, bacon, ham, tinned meat

Heat treatments

Micro-organisms cannot survive at very high temperatures so heat treatments can be an effective method of ensuring food is safe. However, further action – such as sealing the food in sterile containers – is required to prevent re-growth of any harmful organisms. The two main heat treatments used are sterilisation and pasteurisation.

Sterilisation is used in the canned food industry and in the treatment of milk. In the canning process, food is prepared and sealed into cans before being subjected to high temperatures. For low acid food, temperatures used will be between 115°C and 125°C. Cans need to be heated for sufficient time to ensure that every piece of has remained at the required temperature for at least three minutes. This will achieve what is known as 'botulinum cook' which kills the bacteria *Clostridium botulinum*.

The temperature required for sterilisation depends upon the size of the can and the type of food it contains. Larger cans, with denser contents, will require longer cooking times to ensure that all micro-organisms are destroyed. The addition of curing salts to some foods before they are canned can improve the process. Curing salts added to tinned ham, for example, will prevent the growth of bacteria so it is possible to reduce the heat required for sterilisation. This is useful because excessive heat can cause shrinkage of the meat.

Canned foods can be kept at room temperature for long periods as long as the cans remain sealed and undamaged. Once cans are opened, their contents should be treated as perishable foods.

Two different methods are used to sterilise milk. The continuous flow sterilisation process heats milk to between 105°C and 110°C for 20 to 40 minutes. This destroys all micro-organisms and most spores but affects the flavour and nutritional value of the milk. Milk sterilised in this way will keep for at least a week without being refrigerated. Ultra heat treatment (UHT) heats the milk to 132°C for one second, which kills all micro-organisms and their spores. The advantages of this process are that the flavour and nutritional value of the milk are not much affected and the shelf life is considerably lengthened. UHT or 'long life' milk can be kept for at least six months if unopened.

Pasteurisation involves the use of moderate heat to destroy organisms and improve the shelf life of foods. Most commonly used for milk, the method is also used for liquid egg, ice-cream mix and meats. The process does not kill all micro-organisms. Pathogenic bacteria are destroyed, but spoilage organisms and spores remain. Pasteurised foods will require refrigeration in order to prevent new contaminating organisms from growing. Two methods of pasteurisation are used for milk. The holder process holds the milk at between 62.8°C and 65.6°C for 30 minutes, then rapidly cools it to below 10°C. The 'high temperature short time process' heats milk to 71.7°C for 15 seconds then cools it to below 10°C.

FIGURE 3.8

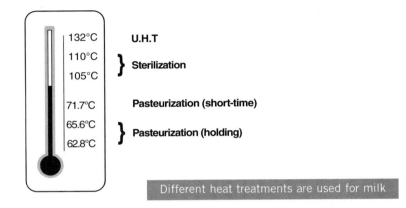

Different heat treatments are used for milk

Reducing temperature

Reducing the temperature of foods generally slows down or stops the growth of micro-organisms. It also slows down the natural spoilage and decay of food, thereby increasing its shelf life. Once the temperature rises again, the organisms will start to grow. Foods can be frozen or chilled. Frozen foods are held at less than 0°C and chilled foods at between 0°C and 5°C.

Freezing controls the growth of micro-organisms in two ways. Firstly, the low temperature slows the growth rate, and secondly, the water in the food turns to ice, making it unavailable to the organisms as moisture. Food needs to be frozen quickly to preserve its texture and appearance. If it is frozen too slowly, large ice crystals form which damage the cell structure of the food. Quick freezing involves reducing the temperature of food from 0°C to –4°C within a very short period (10 minutes to 2 hours, depending on the food). This is the range of temperatures at which most ice crystals form and quick freezing ensures that only small crystals are formed which cause little damage to the food.

The food is prepared prior to freezing by removing unwanted parts and, sometimes, by blanching (rapidly heating for a short time). It will then be frozen using one of the following methods:

▪ Plate freezing – food, for example fish, is compressed between plates filled with refrigerant.

▪ Air blast freezing – a blast of cold air is blown over the food, which is often on a conveyor belt.

- Fluidised bed freezing – a blast of cold air is blown upwards through a moving mesh on which the food is placed. This method is used for small foods such as peas.
- Immersion freezing – the food is placed into the refrigerant. The refrigerant used depends on the food being frozen. Brine may be used for fish, and sugar solutions for fruit and vegetables. Liquid nitrogen is commonly used in modern freezing processes.

Foods are **chilled** at between 0°C and 4°C. Refrigerators, chill cabinets and chill rooms are used to maintain the temperatures of chilled foods. Micro-organism growth is slowed down at these temperatures, although there is concern that some pathogens can still reproduce. These include *Listeria*, and various moulds, for example *Penicillium*.

In **cook–chill** methods, food is cooked then rapidly chilled to less than 3°C within 90 minutes. Chilled foods need to be refrigerated until they are used and re-heated to at least 70°C just prior to serving. Chilled foods can be kept for up to five days.

Cook--freeze methods are similar to cook–chill systems except food is frozen instead of being chilled. This gives a longer shelf life – up to 12 months – but there are problems in maintaining the quality of the food, in ensuring that foods are evenly frozen and in thawing products thoroughly before use.

'Sous-vide' catering uses a combination of preserving methods to improve the safety and extend the shelf life of food. Raw or partially cooked food is packed into vacuum-sealed plastic pouches and pasteurised. The pouches are chilled until required, then re-heated by dropping the bags in boiling water. The pouches can be kept in refrigerated conditions for up to three weeks and give a high quality product. Care is needed to ensure that the acidity level of the food in the pouches is below pH 4.5 so that the growth of *Clostridium botulinum* is prevented.

Excluding oxygen

Many micro-organisms require oxygen in order to grow and reproduce, so by excluding oxygen – by vacuum packing for example – their growth can be inhibited. The method is most effective in controlling moulds and spoilage organisms and is used for hard cheeses and cured meats. It is important to realise that not all bacteria require oxygen and those such as *Clostridium botulinum* will grow in vacuum packs if the acidity level is above pH 4.5.

Oxygen can also be excluded by packing the foods using different gases. Increasing the levels of nitrogen and carbon dioxide and reducing oxygen will inhibit the growth of many micro-organisms. Fish and meat products are packed in this way which is known as 'Controlled or Modified Atmosphere Packing' (CAP/MAP). Foods packaged in this way must, by law, be identified on the label by the term 'packaged in a protective atmosphere'.

Irradiation

Irradiation exposes food to ionising radiation, usually in the form of gamma rays or beams of electrons. The ionising radiation transfers energy to the food particles, generating electrically charged particles which prevent the micro-organisms from growing and reproducing. The method also kills insects. The method can be used on a wide variety of foods though not all foods. It is particularly useful for grains and spices. There are regulations relating to dosage rates and a licence is required from the Ministry for Agriculture, Fisheries and Food to carry out the process.

<table>
</table>

STUDENT ACTIVITY 14

Processes used in preservation of food can be split into three types:

- those that destroy any micro-organisms and then prevent re-growth by sealing the food in protective packaging
- those that limit the growth of micro-organisms by removing one of the growth requirements
- those that limit the growth of bacteria by the addition of chemical preservatives.

Some methods use a combination of the different processes. Identify and briefly describe the processes used to control the growth of micro-organisms in the food.

Control of food pests

In any food premises, steps should be taken to prevent pests gaining entry and breeding. Once pests have infested premises, they are very difficult to remove.

DISCOURAGING PESTS

Rodents

Rodents can be discouraged by:

- ensuring there are no holes in walls, windows, drains, and around where cables or pipes enter the building
- maintaining the areas outside the building by clearing waste and weeds that could act as nest sites
- fixing metal kick plates on doors to prevent rodents gnawing holes
- restricting access to food and water by covering water tanks and storing food off the floor.

Birds

Birds can be discouraged by:

- making all openings into the building bird-proof and filling all holes. Opening may include windows, ventilation apertures and roof spaces
- covering waste and clearing spillage of food.

Insects

Insects can be discouraged by:

- keeping doors and windows screened or closed
- covering all foods in preparation areas and storing food in covered containers
- keeping all food preparation and toilets and washing areas clean and free from waste, cleaning up spillage immediately
- transferring all waste – food and any packaging or other materials – to bins as soon as possible

- keeping waste in covered bins, whether inside or outside the premises and ensuring they are emptied frequently
- placing dustbins off the ground
- checking all incoming food for signs of infestation.

Staff should be aware of the signs of infestation, remain vigilant and report any suspicions of infestation to management.

FIGURES 3.9, 3.10, 3.11 Common pests

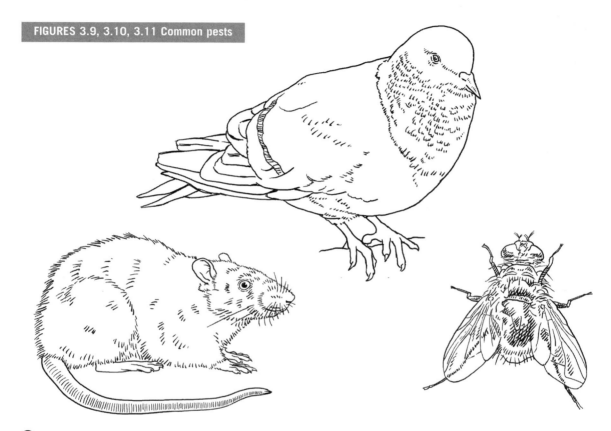

GETTING RID OF PESTS

If pests do gain access to and infest food premises, they will need to be destroyed. This should normally be carried out by experts. They will first assess the extent of the problem before deciding how it should be dealt with.

Infestations will often affect adjoining properties and all properties will need to be treated. Rodents, cockroaches and ants are particularly difficult to eradicate and may require that the premises be closed down during treatment.

The usual method of eradication is by use of chemicals, which can be a hazard in themselves. It is important that they are properly used by trained professionals. Insecticides can be used to kill flying and crawling insects, though they will not kill the eggs of cockroaches. Generally, a second application will be required to kill the newly hatched cockroaches. Electrified ultra violet lights are used in food premises to kill flying insects. Poisons based on anticoagulants are normally used to kill rats and mice. They stop the blood from clotting and cause internal bleeding which is fatal.

 Food Hygiene

STUDENT ACTIVITY 15
Explain which areas in any food premises are most likely to attract pests and why.

Chapter review

This chapter has looked at how the hazards associated with food can be properly controlled. We have looked at general controls for reducing risks from micro-biological, chemical and physical risks. We have considered how pests can be excluded and controlled. We have considered ways of storing and preserving foods to ensure their safety. The next chapter looks at supervisory issues in food premises.

Multiple-choice questions

1   How does freezing work as a method of food preservation?
   A   It kills all the bacteria
   B   It reduces bacteria to a safe level
   C   It stops bacteria reproducing temporarily
   D   It stops bacteria reproducing permanently

2   Which of the following statements is true in relation to cooling foods?
   A   They should be cooled quickly and stored at room temperature
   B   They should be cooled quickly and stored at below 8 °C
   C   They should be cooled slowly and stored at room temperature
   D   They should be cooled in a freezer then allowed to return to room temperature

3   Which of the following statements is true in relation to stock rotation?
   A   Foods purchased first should be used first
   B   Foods purchased first should be used last
   C   Foods purchased last should be used first
   D   Foods can be used in any order

4 Which of the following is *not* a method of preserving food?

    A Cooling

    B Drying

    C Canning

    D Irradiation

5 Which of the following best reflects the temperature at which food in hot holding cabinets should be kept?

    A below 63 °C

    B above 63 °C

    C below 75 °C

    D above 75 °C

6 Which of the following is true about stacking a refrigerator?

    A Raw foods should always be stored on a higher shelf than cooked foods

    B Raw foods should never be stored in a refrigerator

    C Raw foods should be stored at the top of the refrigerator

    D Raw foods should be stored on a lower shelf than cooked foods

7 What is the main reason for not putting hot foods into a freezer with frozen food?

    A Frozen foods may contaminate the hot food with bacteria

    B The hot food may contaminate the frozen food with bacteria

    C The hot food will raise the temperature of the freezer

    D The freezer will cool the hot food too quickly

8 Which of the following is an appropriate temperature for a freezer?

    A −18 °C

    B −15 °C

    C −7 °C

    D −2 °C

9 How should flour be stored?

    A In its original packaging

    B In lidded bins

    C In a suitable cupboard

    D In a warm dry place

Food Hygiene

10 Which of the following could survive treatment with insecticide?

   A Crawling insects

   B Flying insects

   C Cockroaches

   D Cockroach eggs

Short-answer questions

1 Explain how temperature can help to control the growth of micro-organisms.

2 Describe suitable storage conditions for the following items: milk, flour, vegetables, frozen meat.

3 Describe the checks that should be made on incoming deliveries of food items and explain the reasons for these checks.

4 Explain how the different heat treatments can help in ensuring food safety.

5 Explain how pests can be prevented and eliminated from food premises.

4 Supervisory issues

This chapter looks at the supervisor's role in food hygiene. You will learn about:

- the supervisor's role in the management of food hygiene
- the principles and application of Hazard Analysis Critical Control Point (HACCP) systems
- the functions of the Industry Guides to Good Hygiene Practice
- the importance and principles of good standards of personal hygiene
- the importance and methods of good food hygiene and safety training for food handlers
- the principles for selecting hygienic food premises, designing suitable layouts, and installing appropriate equipment
- the importance and methods of cleaning and maintaining food premises.

In previous chapters, you learned about the different risks to food safety. You should understand the importance of minimising those risks. Supervisors in food premises have a legal and moral responsibility to ensure that food is prepared in hygienic conditions. Recent legislation has led to a much more pro-active approach to hygiene management in food premises. Possible hazards should be identified before food safety is affected. Procedures and processes for ensuring food safety must be properly monitored. Most workplaces will have written guidelines and policies relating to food hygiene. Staff will be expected to follow these guidelines and policies. It is important that staff are trained in food hygiene and in specific procedures relating to their workplace. In this chapter, we will consider the supervisor's role in relation to a number of key areas.

Hazard Analysis Critical Control Point Systems (HACCP)

It is important for any food business to identify possible areas of risk and minimise or control them. This is not just out of consideration for their customers, it is also a legal requirement. HACCP is an approach that has been developed to systematically identify food hazards and take action to prevent, minimise or remedy them. There are other approaches, but HACCP is the recommended one and the one used by most food-related businesses in the UK. The aim of HACCP is to focus on potential problems and put in place specific control measures to prevent them occurring. An appropriately qualified person should carry out the analysis.

HACCP PRINCIPLES

The approach has seven principles:

1 Identify the hazards and assess the risks

The first stage is to assess the risk of any hazard occurring in the food-handling processes. This can be done by watching each stage in the food-handling processes. Assessment should cover micro-biological, physical and chemical hazards.

Definitions

Risk: the likelihood that a hazard will occur.

2 Identify critical control points

The next stage is to identify the points in the processes at which hazards can be effectively controlled. These are called the 'critical control points'. The critical control points might be food-handling areas, processes, or practices and procedures which, if not properly controlled, could present risks to the safety of the food.

3 Establish limits for action

Limits need to be set on each of the controls. These will allow staff to make decisions about the safety of food items. Further action needs to be taken when anything occurs that is outside the limits. For example, if freezer temperatures rise above −18°C, action needs to be taken to protect or use the frozen foods.

4 Monitor the controls

It's no good identifying controls if they are not properly monitored. The method of monitoring will depend on the control but might include observation, checking temperatures, checking acidity, checking times, or even taking samples. Monitoring will normally be carried out on batches of food rather than individual food items.

5 Taking corrective action

Monitoring food items should identify areas where the controls are not working. In these areas, action may need to be taken to stop any risks to foods. Action might include discarding some foods, and improving procedures or equipment.

6 Verify the procedure

Two heads are better than one! An appropriate person should be appointed to carry out the assessment of risks. To ensure they have considered all aspects of the food-handling processes, someone else should confirm their findings. This might be another person involved in the business or the local environmental health officer.

7 Documenting the process

Any information about the risk analysis and monitoring process should be accurately recorded. It can help managers analyse the situation if something goes wrong and can also be used to show that the organisation has taken all possible actions to preserve the safety of food. This can be useful in evidence if a legal problem occurs.

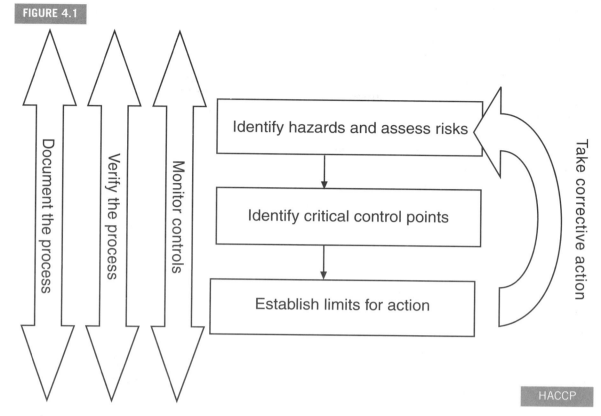

FIGURE 4.1

Identify hazards and assess risks

Identify critical control points

Establish limits for action

Document the process

Verify the process

Monitor controls

Take corrective action

HACCP

IMPLEMENTING HACCP

The implementation of HACCP will depend upon the type and size of food business, but there are some basic steps which will need to be taken in most cases.

Planning

The introduction of HACCP should be carefully planned. This will help to ensure that interruptions to normal work are minimised, and that staff have time to adjust to new procedures. Staff support is essential if the system is to work effectively.

Appointment of suitable persons

A suitably qualified person should be asked to take charge of the inspection procedure. Managers, particularly in larger establishments, may wish to use a small team of people with experience of different areas of the business to ensure that all aspects are properly covered.

Documenting operations

All operations should be documented. This involves identifying and describing all food-handling operations. Processes can be documented by use of a flowchart. Computer software is now available to make the flowcharting of operations easier.

The flowchart in Figure 4.2 shows the operations involved in making an omelette.

FIGURE 4.2

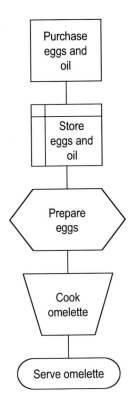

Purchase eggs and oil

Store eggs and oil

Prepare eggs

Cook omelette

Serve omelette

Making an omelette

 STUDENT ACTIVITY 16
Draw a flowchart of food-handling operations for making a ham sandwich.

Introducing HACCP

When the above steps have been completed, the appointed person(s) works through the HACCP principles. This will involve identifying hazards, assessing risks, identifying controls, setting limits, designing procedures, appointing responsible persons for inspection and monitoring, and designing recording systems. For each stage in food handling, they should consider what happens to the food, what are the likely contaminants, and what will happen to the food next. This will help them to decide the controls required to ensure that food moves to the next stage in an appropriate state. The team will need to decide, for each stage, whether the hazard can be eliminated or minimised at that point or at a later stage.

Table 4.1 shows the hazards, controls and monitoring checks required for the processes involved in making an omelette.

 STUDENT ACTIVITY 17
For the ham sandwich flowchart you constructed in the last activity, prepare a table showing hazards, controls and monitoring checks.

Table 4.1 Making an omelette

Steps in the process	Hazards What can go wrong?	Controls What can I do about it?	Monitor How can I check?
Purchase of eggs and oil	• Bought ingredients contaminated with bacteria, mould or foreign bodies • Ingredients could be contaminated during delivery • Ingredients could be at inappropriate temperature on delivery	• Use reputable suppliers for eggs Use eggs with 'lion' standard mark • Check goods on receipt for damage	• Check delivery vehicles • Check date marks • Check temperatures • Check food condition
Store eggs and oil	• Contamination could take place during storage • Cross-contamination could take place during storage	• Store eggs in the fridge • Use proper stock rotation – First in, First out • Store oil in cool, dry place	• Check storage temperatures • Check storage conditions
Prepare eggs	• Contamination or cross-contamination from other foods, food handlers, utensils or equipment	• Limit handling • Good personal hygiene of food handlers • Food handlers properly trained • Surfaces and utensils clean • Use clean bowls and utensils to prepare eggs	• Visual checks on food areas, food handlers, etc. • Cleaning schedules
Cook omelette	• Survival of harmful bacteria	• Make sure eggs are cooked through	• Visual check • Cooking times
Serve omelette	• Contamination before serving	• Serving areas clean • Food served immediately • Good personal hygiene of serving staff • No contact between raw and cooked foods	• Visual checks of food, food areas and procedures (check food not left before serving)

Checking the system

Once the system is in place, checks should be made to ensure that it is operating properly, and that staff are aware of their responsibilities. Full reviews of the system should be carried out periodically to ensure all procedures are working as intended. Modifications may need to be made especially where changes in processes have taken place or where the procedures are unworkable for some reason. Note that these checks are separate from the general monitoring that will take place on a day-to-day basis.

Businesses such as food processing plants will find the introduction of HACCP relatively straightforward. It is likely that the raw materials are not very varied and processing is standardised. It is harder for many catering establishments who may deal with a wide range of different foods – some raw, some ready to eat – and processes such as thawing, preparing, cooking, storing, serving. Table 4.2 shows examples of the hazards that can occur in these types of establishment and the actions that can be taken to control them. (Note that the table is not meant to be exhaustive, but highlights common hazards.)

Table 4.2 Suitable controls in food-handling operations

Stage	Hazard	Risks	Actions
Purchase	• Incoming deliveries already contaminated, or damaged during delivery • Temperatures may not comply with legal requirements	• Food already contaminated with pathogens • Growth of pathogens	• Purchase from reputable suppliers • Agree delivery temperatures with suppliers
Receipt	• Temperatures may not comply with legal requirements • May be close to, or out of date • Damaged packaging or foodstuffs (e.g. blown cans, cracked eggs)	• Growth of pathogens • Spoilage of food has begun • Micro-biological, physical space or chemical contaminants	• Check temperatures on arrival and reject any items not at required temperatures • Check best before/use by dates • Check packaging for damage and don't accept damaged goods
Storage	• Temperatures may not comply with legal requirements • Raw and cooked foods stored together • Out of date foods at back of storage areas • Contamination by non-food items	• Growth of pathogens • Cross-contamination • Spoiled foods • Physical/chemical contamination	• Check storage temperatures frequently to ensure they are within correct range • Store raw and cooked foods separately • Use proper stock rotation system • Store non-food items separately
Preparation	• Food kept too long at room temperature • Handling of raw and cooked foods without washing hands • Infrequent washing of hands • Multiple uses for sinks, equipment etc leading to cross-contamination • Dirty and badly maintained equipment and utensils • Foods washed in contaminated water	• Growth of pathogens • Cross-contamination • Physical contamination from damaged equipment	• Keep food at room temperature for minimum time • Wash hands between handling raw and cooked foods • Wash hands frequently • Separate sinks for dishes, food and hands • Keep equipment and utensils clean and in good repair • Ensure water supply is not contaminated
Cooking	• Undercooked food, especially meat • Temperatures for cooking or re-heating not adequate to destroy all pathogens • Frozen food not properly thawed • Handling of cooked foods • Handling raw foods and cooked foods • Surfaces and equipment used for raw and cooked foods • Handlers improperly dressed	• Growth of pathogens • Pathogens not destroyed • Cross-contamination • Physical contaminants from clothes/body of handlers	• Cook or re-heat for appropriate times at appropriate temperatures in order to cook through and kill organisms • Allow time to thaw frozen foods fully before cooking • Use gloves to handle cooked foods where possible • Wearing of proper protective clothing

Table 4.2 Suitable controls in food-handling operations – continued

Stage	Hazard	Risks	Actions
Cooling	• Unsuitable containers used for cooling • Foods not cooled quickly enough • Design or temperatures of chill cabinets inadequate	• Growth of pathogens • Production of toxins	• Use shallow containers that are not too large for cooling • Use a blast chiller if available or cool as quickly as possible • Check temperatures and instructions for use of chill cabinets
Hot holding	• Hot holding cabinets not hot enough • Foods held for too long at wrong temperature	• Growth of pathogens • Production of toxins	• Keep food at temperatures above 63 °C to prevent growth of organisms • Don't hold foods for long periods
Chilled storage	• Wrong temperatures used to hold perishable food • Food left uncovered in display cabinets	• Growth of pathogens	• Ensure chilled storage is at 8 °C or below, or lower if required by specific foods • Cover foods
Serving	• Foods left too long before serving	• Growth of pathogens • Production of toxins • Cross-contamination	• Serve foods immediately on cooking, re-heating or removal from chilled storage

Guides to good practice

There are a number of guides published to help managers identify and eliminate hazards in their food businesses. The DoH produces a general guide to food hazards and a booklet called *Assured Safe Catering* which explains how the principles of HACCP can be introduced into a business. Managers should also obtain the relevant Industry Guides to Good Hygiene Practice. These have been produced by trade associations along guidelines set out by the DoH to provide a framework of good practice within which businesses can operate. Managers should also be aware of new issues arising in relation to their own area of work and obtain any relevant information including government reports.

Personal hygiene

Most food-related illness is due to people. It may be they are unknowing carriers of an illness that can be transmitted by food, or that they are not careful enough in the way they handle and prepare food. The human body acts as a habitat and as a vehicle for all sorts of micro-organisms, some of which are harmless and others which are not. Good personal hygiene will help to minimise the risks of contaminating food and is the legal responsibility of every food handler. Supervisors and managers need to train and motivate staff and set the right sort of example to them.

It is important that food handlers are generally clean and tidy, wear appropriate protective clothing and avoid wearing heavy make-up, nail varnish, hair ornaments and jewellery which could harbour micro-organisms or fall off and contaminate food.

 STUDENT ACTIVITY 18
List the ways in which a food handler might transfer micro-organisms to food.

Handwashing

The most likely vehicle for micro-organisms is the hands. Hands should be washed frequently, and handlers should avoid touching food with the hands as much as possible.

 Handwashing is generally one of the most neglected areas of hygienic food operations. It's no good taking all the right steps to protect food if you then prepare it with dirty hands! If in doubt – wash them!

Hands should always be washed:

▮ before starting work and handling food
▮ between handling raw and cooked foods
▮ after handling raw food
▮ before handling cooked foods
▮ after handling dirty equipment
▮ after going to the toilet
▮ after smoking, drinking or eating
▮ after combing or touching the hair
▮ after sneezing, blowing the nose, or touching the face
▮ after handling refuse
▮ after cleaning or touching cleaning chemicals.

Hands should be washed with hot water and un-perfumed soap and dried thoroughly using paper or roller towels. Liquid soap is preferable as bar soap can lead to contamination.

UNHYGIENIC HABITS

Food handlers also need to avoid any bad habits that could lead to contamination such as:

▮ picking their nose
▮ biting their nails
▮ licking their fingers
▮ spitting
▮ dipping fingers into food

- smoking
- coughing or sneezing over food
- blowing on food
- using a spoon to test food but failing to wash it between tastings
- blowing on glass or silverware to polish it
- eating and drinking in food-handling areas.

Staff illness

It is important that staff do not handle food when suffering from certain symptoms or illnesses. The DoH has issued guidance about illness of food handlers and the actions that should be taken (*Food Handlers: Fitness to Work*). Staff should be made aware that they need to report the following symptoms:

- food poisoning or related symptoms, e.g. vomiting and diarrhoea suffered by yourself or a member of your family
- heavy colds or flu
- cuts, wounds or spots that have become septic.

You should report vomiting and diarrhoea in family members to an employer even if you are not feeling ill. It is possible to be a carrier without having the symptoms yourself.

Handlers also need to inform their superiors if they suspect that, as a result of an earlier illness, they might be a carrier of a disease that can be transmitted by food. They should tell their doctor that they are a food handler when being treated for any illness involving stomach or bowel problems. Doctors will be able to identify risk in specific cases.

Managers should ensure that staff suffering from any of these symptoms are removed from food-handling duties. The DoH recommends that managers in food businesses notify the Consultant in Communicable Disease Control and the local Environmental Health Department if any member of staff reports food-borne illness or infection.

First aid

Skin wounds should generally be covered with a clean, waterproof dressing. Dressings for use by food handlers are generally dark blue to minimise the risk of them falling unnoticed into foods. Employers should provide antiseptic wipes for cleaning wounds. There should be a trained first aider who can apply immediate aid for anyone injured or

taken ill. Training should include how to deal with cuts and other wounds, burns and chemical irritation of skin or eyes.

Protective clothing

Staff dress in a food-handling area should always be appropriate. They should wear appropriate protective clothing to prevent food becoming contaminated. Staff should not wear jewellery, perfume or nail varnish. Protective clothing includes overalls, hair nets, head coverings and, where appropriate, gloves and aprons. It should always be kept clean.

PHOTOGRAPH 4.1

Appropriate dress in the kitchen is important

Some measures to protect food from contamination by handlers include:

■ covering hair and beards to prevent hair, and the micro-organisms that live on it, from coming into contact with food

■ wearing aprons, either disposable or washable, where dirty tasks are undertaken or additional protection is required, for example in butchery trades when cutting up meat or poultry

■ wearing rubber or disposable gloves for further protection for specific food-handling and cleaning tasks

■ wearing non-slip footwear and waterproof footwear in wet areas.

All clothing should be light coloured to show dirt, washable, in good condition and should only be worn in the food-handling area and never outside. Torn or frayed clothing does not only look untidy but can present food hazards especially if fastenings or pieces of clothing could become detached and contaminate food. Specifically, waiting staff should wear clothing that distinguishes them from other staff and chefs' clothing should completely cover their own underclothes. Clean and dirty clothing should be stored in separate places provided by the company.

As with personal hygiene, managers should set the right example to staff by wearing appropriate clothing themselves. Staff should receive appropriate training in hygienic practices and these practices should be monitored as part of the HACCP system. Staff should always be advised when their appearance, clothing or habits are inappropriate for food handling.

STUDENT ACTIVITY 19

Explain the hazards that might arise from incorrect dress in food-handling areas.

Hygiene training

By law, all food handlers are required to have some food hygiene training. Managers should ensure that training is updated at appropriate intervals or when changes in role, tasks or processes require it.

Training should cover all general aspects of food hygiene including the causes and prevention of food-borne illness. Staff should understand enough about microbiology to realise why the procedures they are required to follow are necessary. Staff will always be more motivated to follow procedures if they have an understanding of the reasons behind them.

Managers should ensure that all training is carried out at the appropriate level, using methods suited to the staff who are being trained. For example, technical and scientific terms should be avoided until it is ascertained that staff are familiar with these. Updates will be required at regular intervals and also in relation to specific new roles, processes, tasks or products. As well as training courses, 'on the job' instruction will help staff understand the importance of hygienic practices specifically in relation to their own role. For small businesses, local environmental health offices and expert training organisations may be able to offer help and advice on training.

Managers and supervisors will need to ensure that records are kept of the level, coverage and date of training for each member of staff. This will provide evidence that the legal obligation to train food handlers has been met, and will provide a reference for keeping training up to date and relevant.

DID YOU KNOW ?

As a manager or supervisor in a food business, you would be responsible for making sure all your staff were properly trained. There are lots of organisations that provide basic food hygiene training. You could try local colleges or specialist training organisations. Qualifications in food hygiene are offered by a number of awarding bodies such as the Chartered Institute of Environmental Health and the Royal Institute of Public Health.

Design and construction of food premises and equipment

Food premises are defined in legislation as any site where food is prepared, stored or sold. This includes a wide variety of organisations at every stage of the food chain – production, processing, preparing, serving and selling.

STUDENT ACTIVITY 20

For each of the following, give two examples of food premises which might carry out these activities with food:

▪ production
▪ processing
▪ preparation
▪ serving
▪ selling.

Most new food businesses will set up in existing premises converted for the purpose. A few will be in the position of designing and building food premises from scratch. Whatever the situation, food hygiene is a principal concern when designing and constructing food premises. Every different food business will present its own challenges and problems in relation to design, but there are mandatory requirements in the hygienic design of food premises which need to be applied. Up-to-date regulations and guidance on design and construction of food premises should always be consulted before any construction or improvement work takes place. The legal requirements are explained in Chapter 5. In this chapter we will consider the principles of hygienic design.

SITE

Considerations when choosing a suitable site for any food premises include the following:

▪ access to the site for staff, for deliveries of raw materials, distribution of the product, where appropriate, and removal of waste
▪ provision of mains gas, electricity and telephone as well as a clean water supply and sufficient sewage disposal facilities

- possible contamination by industrial fumes, dust or smoke, refuse sites, derelict areas, or by flooding.

Water supplies need to be appropriate to usage. In particular, water which will be used for drinking, washing and preparing food, and cleaning food contact surfaces and equipment must comply with microbiological and toxicological standards set out by law. Hot and cold running water should be available and hot water should be at least 60 °C for washing surfaces and equipment, and 50 °C for hand washing. Where water has to be stored in tanks, it will need to be checked regularly for contamination by micro-organisms. Tanks should be covered, regularly emptied and cleaned, and may need to be chlorinated. Water not intended for drinking should not be allowed to contaminate drinking water or food preparation areas.

Premises should be sited where risks to hygiene are minimised. In addition, the impact of the food premises on the local area should be assessed, as this will avoid any disputes at later dates. Food premises can be noisy operations and may operate at unsociable hours and even throughout the night. Siting the premises where they will cause minimum disruption to others might avoid complaints at a later date.

DESIGN

Design of premises should allow for hygienic operations. A good starting point in design is to consider the critical control points relating to the specific food business. Premises can then be designed to make it easier to put controls in place. Considerations should be as follows:

- Work flow – food should move from its raw, dirty state, to the finished state in which it is sold or served to customers. Ideally, design of premises should take account of this progression and physically move food from its raw state at one end of the premises, through processing areas, to its finished state at the other end. Keeping clean and dirty processes apart will help to reduce the risk of cross-contamination, as will keeping cooked foods separate from raw ingredients. Where possible, physical barriers should be used. Work flow should allow for food to move quickly through the processing stages, minimising the time that it is left at room temperature.

FIGURE 4.3

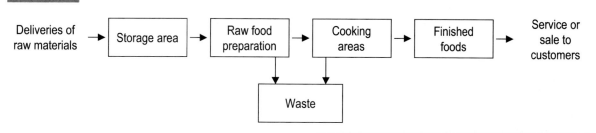

Premises should be designed around work flow

- Space – food premises should have sufficient space for each separate food-processing task. Premises that are overcrowded with insufficient space for equipment and for staff to work, encourage unhygienic habits and insufficient care over cleaning

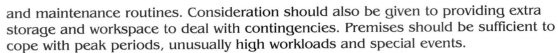

and maintenance routines. Consideration should also be given to providing extra storage and workspace to deal with contingencies. Premises should be sufficient to cope with peak periods, unusually high workloads and special events.

- Cleaning – premises will need to be frequently cleaned and design should allow for this. Surfaces should be constructed from materials that are hygienic and easy to clean, and all areas should be easily accessible for cleaning.

- Pests – we looked at pest control in Chapter 3 and saw that the best way to minimise risks was to avoid infestation. Premises should be designed to restrict access to rodents, insects and birds. Areas outside the building, especially waste areas, should be kept clean, and clear of weeds.

- Storage areas – suitable storage areas will need to be provided for each different type of food used on the premises. This may include dry storage areas, and cold stores. Storage will also need to be provided for cleaning and maintenance materials and equipment, refuse, and the personal belongings, clothes, etc. of staff. Refrigerators and cold stores will need to be sited in areas with sufficient ventilation and away from heat sources. All storage should give easy access for cleaning.

- Hygiene facilities – sufficient and appropriate toilet and washing facilities need to be provided for all members of staff by law. The number of type of facilities will depend on the size and activities of the business. General rules for toilet facilities include separation from food preparation areas by a ventilated passage or space; notices in toilets to remind staff to wash their hands, wash hand basins with hot and cold water and suitable soap; hot air hand dryers, roller towels or paper towels. Hand washing and drying facilities also need to be provided close to food preparation areas. Staff changing facilities need to be situated with easy access to food preparation areas to minimise the risk of contamination.

- Ventilation – food premises need to be well ventilated to reduce the build up of heat and odours. In most cases natural ventilation will not be sufficient and some mechanical help is required. This might include oven canopies, fans and filter systems. Any ventilation openings will need screens to prevent pests gaining entry.

- Lighting – good lighting is essential to make working conditions safer, to allow thorough cleaning, and to discourage pests – particularly rodents who dislike bright lights.

- Refuse disposal – premises design will need to allow for the hygienic disposal of all refuse. Waste disposal units will help disposal of some food waste. Other waste from food areas should be collected in plastic sacks and removed from the area as soon as possible. External waste storage areas should be paved, with lidded bins that are raised above ground level. Facilities for washing the area will need to be available.

CONSTRUCTION

Buildings should be constructed of suitable materials and to a design that is waterproof and minimises access for pests. Walls and foundations should be solidly built, avoiding spaces which could harbour pests, and roof design should be such that it does not provide roosting sites or pooled water which may attract birds. Internally all surfaces should have non-absorbent coverings and be free from cracks and crevices in which dirt could collect. They should be sealed at junctions between ceilings, walls and floors and should be smooth to allow for easy cleaning. Specific considerations include:

- Floor surfaces – should be hard-wearing, non-slip, and designed so that any water drains away into drainage gullies.

- Drainage – gullies should be smooth and curved for ease of cleaning, and drains should be able to cope at all work levels without overflowing. Grease traps will avoid significant amounts of fat being discharged into the drainage system and grids. Covers and traps on equipment drains will help hygiene and prevent access by pests.

- Internal wall surfaces – should be easily cleaned and resistant to hot fat, or being knocked by trolleys where appropriate. They should be light coloured to aid cleaning and properly maintained so that there are no cracks.

- Ceilings – should also be washable and should be at a suitable height to allow adequate ventilation. Where the processes produce steam, absorbent surfaces will help to avoid condensation and dripping. Suspended ceilings should allow easy access for inspection and cleaning.

- Doors – should be washable with durable surfaces, and fit closely to restrict access for pests. They will need to open wide enough to move equipment and be self-closing.

EQUIPMENT

Equipment in food premises may have to be moved and/or dismantled to allow for thorough cleaning. Design of equipment and the areas where it is sited will need to allow for these cleaning operations to take place. There should be sufficient equipment to cope with the work levels and it should be of a suitable standard to cope with the demands of industrial use. Domestic equipment will not normally be suitable.

Equipment should be designed so that:

- any surfaces do not react with food and drink or absorb any liquids
- it is easy to clean and there are no cracks or crevices where food could collect or pests could hide
- it is easy to maintain and repair
- the food is protected from the external environment
- it is mobile, where possible, so it can be moved for cleaning.

Premises and equipment should be regularly checked for damage and wear, and well maintained.

Cleaning

STUDENT ACTIVITY 21
Say why you think cleaning is important in food premises and list areas you think should be regularly cleaned.

Cleaning is an essential part of any food-related operation. Owners and managers of these operations have a legal responsibility to ensure premises and equipment are kept clean and in good repair, but everyone in food establishments needs to take some responsibility for ensuring high standards of cleanliness are maintained. Food debris can harbour pathogenic bacteria, contaminate food and attract pests; and dirty premises are guaranteed to discourage customers. Cleaning and disinfecting will help to reduce the hazards associated with food debris. Cleaning staff will carry out many tasks, but all staff members should take some responsibility for ensuring that the equipment and areas in which they work are clean. Cleaning is achieved by physical effort – by people or machines – by the use of hot water, and by the use of chemicals.

Definitions

Cleaning: the process of removing dirt

Disinfection: destruction of micro-organisms to a level not hazardous to health or likely to cause food spoilage

STAGES OF CLEANING AND DISINFECTION

There are a number of stages to the cleaning process, whether cleaning surfaces, equipment or utensils.

1 *Pre-clean* – This involves removing any loose dirt and heavy soiling. Examples are soaking cooking pots and pans, scraping plates, wiping down surfaces and sweeping floors.

2 *Clean* – This stage involves washing the equipment, utensils or surfaces with hot water and detergent. A suitable cloth or brush should be used in order to remove grease and dirt effectively.

3 *Rinse* – The rinse stage is to remove any detergent and remaining dirt. Rinsing should be done with hot water.

4 *Disinfect* – Disinfecting can be achieved with chemical disinfectants or hot water. Chemical disinfectants should be appropriate for the purpose and the manufacturer's instructions must be followed. If disinfecting is done using hot water, the water needs to be heated to above 82 °C. Disinfecting will ensure that micro-organisms are reduced to safe levels.

5 *Final rinse* – The final rinse will make sure that any remaining detergents or cleaning fluids are removed. It should be done using clean, hot water.

6 *Dry* – Air drying is the most hygienic method of drying. Drying cloths can spread micro-organisms. If it is not possible to air dry, then use absorbent disposable towels.

7 *Clean and store cleaning equipment* – Any brushes, cloths, mops, etc. used for cleaning should be cleaned and disinfected. Disposable cloths should be thrown away. All equipment and chemicals should be returned to their appropriate storage areas.

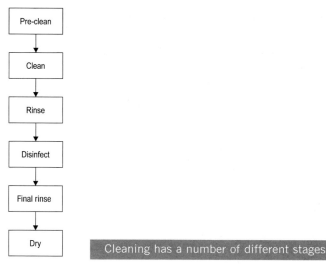

Cleaning has a number of different stages

Not all surfaces and equipment require disinfection. Disinfection is appropriate for:

- food contact surfaces such as work surfaces and chopping boards
- hand contact surfaces such as door handles
- cleaning materials and equipment.

Cleaning should be carried out before dirt and food have had time to harden on the surfaces as this will stop micro-organisms growing and multiplying, and make the job easier.

CLEANING SCHEDULES

Every food-handling operation should have a written cleaning schedule. The cleaning schedule should identify:

- all equipment, utensils, surfaces and areas that need cleaning and disinfection
- how often each of the above should be cleaned and disinfected
- when cleaning and disinfecting should be carried out in each case including during food preparation, after food preparation and when spillage occurs
- the persons responsible for each cleaning task
- methods and materials that are to be used for each cleaning task, including the amounts and types of chemicals to be used for each task
- any safety precautions that need to be considered with regard to the method of cleaning, the items being cleaned and the cleaning chemicals and equipment used.

The objectives of a cleaning schedule are to ensure that cleaning is carried out as efficiently as possible, follows a routine, and uses a minimum number of cleaning chemicals. When preparing the schedule, the areas and equipment to be cleaned must be considered so that appropriate cleaning materials are provided.

Equipment instructions should be checked to establish how each piece is to be cleaned. Some equipment will need to be cleaned where it stands because it is too large and/or difficult to dismantle. This is known as 'cleaning-in-place'.

Cleaning-in-place occurs particularly in the brewing, soft drinks and dairy industries where the equipment cannot be dismantled every time cleaning is required. Special non-foaming detergents and disinfectants are used to clean equipment and pipework by circulating them through the system. A basic clean-in-place procedure will have the following stages:

I circulate cold water through the system to remove loose dirt
I circulate detergent to remove remaining dirt
I circulate disinfectant to destroy micro-organisms
I circulate clean cold water to remove any remaining disinfectant.

Managers will need to ensure that there are adequate cleaning staff and that they are provided with appropriate materials and equipment. Cleaning operations should be carefully planned and should not disrupt food production or contaminate food. All cleaning staff should be aware of the following:

I all food should be removed from the area to be cleaned and stored in a suitable place
I any electrical equipment should be switched off and disconnected before being cleaned
I any chemicals should be used only according to the manufacturer's instructions
I appropriate protective clothing should be worn for all cleaning tasks
I the set procedures for all cleaning tasks should be followed.

EQUIPMENT FOR CLEANING

Cloths and traditional string mops provide breeding grounds for bacteria and, if used, need frequent washing and soaking in disinfectants. Sponge mops and brushes provide a safer alternative for floors, and disposable cloths or specially designed wipers can be used on surfaces. Different coloured equipment can be used for separate cleaning areas to reduce the risk of cross-contamination. All equipment should be washed between uses and sterilised.

Many food businesses now use dishwashing machines to clean pots, cutlery and utensils, and glass washing machines are often used in pubs and restaurants. These generally wash by spraying jets of water on to the contents, and usually rinse at above 82°C to disinfect, though some glass washing machines use revolving brushes. Any dried-on food will need to be removed before placing in the dishwasher. As with any equipment, the manufacturer's instructions should always be followed, recommended detergents should be used, and machines should be regularly checked and serviced.

Where washing-up is carried out manually, the two sink system is most effective. One sink is used for washing and the other for rinsing in hot water to disinfect. Washing should use water at about 60°C and the correct quantity of a suitable detergent. Rinsing should be carried out at 82°C or above and the water in the rinsing sink will need to be replaced frequently to keep it at the correct temperature. Rubber gloves will protect hands from the hot water. Soaking items for a short time may help to remove any food that has dried. Pots, cutlery and utensils should be left to air dry as drying cloths can carry bacteria.

PHOTOGRAPH 4.2

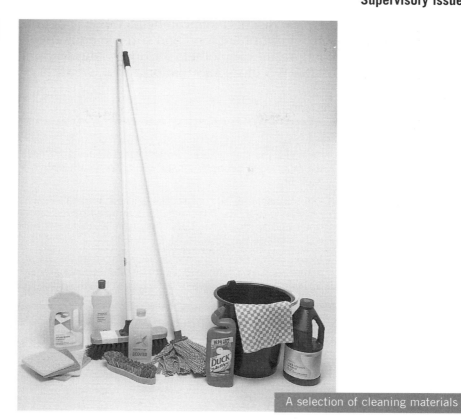

A selection of cleaning materials

CLEANING CHEMICALS

Many different chemicals are used in cleaning and it is important that the right chemical is used for each cleaning job. It is also important that they are used correctly and not allowed to contaminate food. The use of chemicals for cleaning is controlled by the Control of Substances Hazardous to Health Regulations 1994 which we will consider along with other legislation in Chapter 5. Here we will look at the different chemical cleaners and their uses.

Detergents are used to remove grease and dirt by enabling the grease to dissolve in the water. They also soften the water, making it easier to use. They can be acid- or alkali-based. Most general purpose detergents are alkaline. Acid detergents are usually used for specific purposes. Detergents should never be mixed, and this can have quite serious results where acids and alkali solutions are mixed as toxic fumes may be released. Detergents will work better in hot water.

Strong acids and **alkalis** are sometimes used for special purpose cleaning:

■ caustic soda (alkali) is used for oven cleaning as it will remove burnt-on grease
■ strong acids such as sulphamic or phosphoric are used to remove limescale.

These strong acids and alkalis should never be allowed to come into contact with the skin as they will cause severe irritation. Fumes can also irritate the eyes.

Disinfectants will destroy micro-organisms to an acceptable level but will not destroy their spores. Water at 82 °C or above acts as a disinfectant. However, hot water cannot

CORNWALL COLLEGE
LEARNING CENTRE

always be used so chemical disinfectants can help. These should be chosen with care as some are poisonous and can taint food and corrode equipment. Hypochlorites are most often used by food businesses; others include quaternary ammonium compounds (QACs) and phenols. Table 4.3 gives information about chemical disinfectants.

Table 4.3 Chemical disinfectants

Hypochlorites	Oxidising agents that kill germs by oxidising them. They kill bacteria and destroy some spores, are harmless, and are cheap. Effectiveness is reduced by too much food debris and hard water. They can corrode metals and have a short shelf life.
QACs and diguanides	Will kill bacteria, but not spores, and some micro-organisms can develop a resistance to them. Effectiveness is reduced by too much food debris, hard water and artificial materials. They have a longer shelf life than the hypochlorites.
Phenols	More effective against some bacteria, for example *Staphylococcus aureus*, than others such as *Salmonella*. Do not destroy spores and are seriously inactivated by large amounts of food debris and hard water. Also, can taint food.

Sanitisers are a combination of detergents and disinfectants and kill micro-organisms while removing dirt. However, it is usually better to make two applications.

 STUDENT ACTIVITY 22
List the responsibilities of managers and supervisors with regard to cleaning.

Chapter review

This chapter has looked at the supervisory aspects of food hygiene and safety. It is the responsibility of managers and supervisors to ensure the hygiene of staff and premises. In this chapter you have learned how managers can assess the risks and put controls in place to reduce them. You have also considered aspects of personal hygiene, design of premises and cleaning of premises. The next chapter introduces laws relating to food hygiene and safety.

Multiple-choice questions

1   Why should food handlers wear protective clothing?
    A   To prevent clothes from becoming contaminated
    B   To prevent food from becoming contaminated
    C   To protect own clothes from spills
    D   To keep them warm in cold storage areas

2   Why is it important to tell your employer about symptoms of food-related illness among your family members even if you are not ill yourself?
    A   Because you could be a carrier of the illness without knowing
    B   Because you may become ill at work
    C   In case you need to go home suddenly
    D   In case it was caused by food prepared by you

3   In which of the following situations should you wash your hands?
    A   Before smoking a cigarette
    B   After cleaning
    C   Before handling raw eggs in their shells
    D   All of the above

4   Which of the following is important to consider when designing premises for food handling?
    A   Adequate space for food preparation
    B   Separation of clean and dirty tasks
    C   Prevention of pest infestation
    D   All of the above

5   What is the main purpose of HACCP?
    A   To document food-handling operations
    B   To identify where food hygiene is going wrong
    C   To identify food hazards and prevent or minimise them
    D   To ensure food handlers comply with set procedures

6   What is the purpose of disinfecting equipment, utensils or surfaces?
   A   To kill all micro-organisms
   B   To reduce micro-organisms to a safe level
   C   To remove surface dirt
   D   To remove food particles

7   What is the difference between cleaning and disinfecting?
   A   They are used for different areas and equipment
   B   Chemicals are used for disinfecting but not for cleaning
   C   Cleaning removes dirt and disinfecting reduces bacteria
   D   Cleaning removes dirt and disinfecting kills all bacteria

8   Which of the following would be the greatest risk to food safety?
   A   A broken finger
   B   A large bruise on the arm
   C   A broken fingernail
   D   A wound on the hand

9   Which of the following best describes the stages of cleaning and disinfection?
   A   Pre-clean, clean, rinse, disinfect, final rinse, dry
   B   Pre-clean, rinse, clean, disinfect, final rinse, dry
   C   Rinse, pre-clean, clean, disinfect, final rinse, dry
   D   Pre-clean, disinfect, rinse, clean, final rinse, dry

10   Why are wound dressings for food handlers coloured blue?
   A   To distinguish them from dressings for other people
   B   Because they have a special antibacterial coating
   C   So managers can see handlers are injured
   D   So they can be seen if they fall into food

Short-answer questions

1 Explain what HACCP means and how it is used in the workplace.

2 Give three examples of critical control points in a food preparation or service situation and identify appropriate measures to ensure food safety.

3 Describe the qualities of protective clothing for food handlers and the reasons that it is worn.

4 Explain the importance of personal hygiene for food handlers and identify elements of good personal hygiene.

5 Explain how cleaning should be carried out in food establishments and describe the equipment and materials used.

5 Food law

Sources of food law

UK law comes from a variety of sources. Laws about food hygiene come from:

■ European Directives
■ Acts of the UK Parliament
■ regulations
■ Codes of Practice relating to food safety.

Each of these is described in more detail below.

FIGURE 5.1

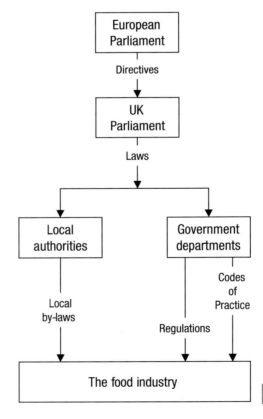

The sources of food hygiene law

European Directives

The UK is part of the European Union (EU). As such, it is subject to regulations made by the European Commission and the Council of Ministers. Guidelines on food safety have been in the form of European Directives. These instruct member states to introduce laws or to change their existing laws to cover any areas agreed by the EU. European Directives do not become law in this country until they have been confirmed by our own Parliament.

Acts of Parliament

UK law is made by the UK Parliament. A 'bill' (a sort of draft of the law) is presented to Parliament for consideration. It is voted on by the members of the House of Commons and the House of Lords. It becomes law if a majority of votes are in favour.

Laws relating to food safety are usually 'enabling' acts. An enabling act sets out the main principles of the required law but gives power to Government agencies to design the detailed framework by which the law is put into practice. Government agencies include the Civil Service and local authorities.

Regulations

Acts of Parliament can authorise Government departments to draw up regulations. Regulations explain the way that the Act is to be interpreted. These regulations then become part of the law. This is useful because it means minor changes can be made quickly to cover new situations without changes to the main legislation.

Codes of Practice

Under the Food Safety Act, Government departments can issue Codes of Practice that explain how regulations will be enforced, and recommend standards for consistency of enforcement.

The first *Recommended International Code of Practice on the General Principles of Food Hygiene* was published in 1969 by the Joint Commission of the Food and Agriculture Organisation and the World Health Organisation. The provisions of this Code of Practice are now included in more recent food safety legislation.

Local by-laws

These are local laws made by local authorities and are only applicable in the authorities' local area. They must be approved by a minister before they become law.

In the late 1980s, there was much concern about food safety following a number of food scares. The Government started to legislate to ensure food safety, at the same time taking account of European Directives related to food safety. There are many regulations relating to all areas of food safety. We will look at some of the more common areas here.

The Food Safety Act 1990

The Food Safety Act was passed in 1990 in response to public concern over the safety of food. The aim of the Act is to control food safety at all stages of production. It is a criminal offence not to comply with the Act. The Act details powers of enforcement and penalties for non-compliance. The Act is also an enabling Act, allowing ministers to make regulations detailing requirements under the Act.

It is important that legislation is clear and cannot be misinterpreted so the Act contains a definition of food. The definition of food under the Act includes any drinks, articles and substances used for human consumption, or used as ingredients in the preparation of food, as well as chewing gum and similar products, and fish that are eaten live, for example, oysters.

The Act applies to any food supplied in the course of a business or offered as a prize or reward. In case of any dispute, the Act states that it will be assumed that any foods found on food premises, which would normally be consumed by humans, are for supply to customers.

OFFENCES UNDER THE ACT

There are four main offences under the Act:

■ making food injurious to health either deliberately or accidentally
■ selling food that does not comply with food safety requirements being unfit for human consumption or contaminated
■ selling food which is not of the nature or substance or quality required by the consumer
■ falsely describing, advertising or labelling food and food products.

ENFORCEMENT OF THE ACT

Local environmental health officers enforce the Act. They are given the power to enter food premises and take samples of food for analysis. Management and empoyees are required to co-operate with officers.

Officers can gain entry at any reasonable time but must produce a document showing authority if requested. Samples may be subjected to:

■ chemical analysis to establish their contents in order to check labelling
■ microbiological examination to check suitability for consumption.

NOTICES AND ORDERS

Where they find a problem with food premises, environmental health officers can issue the following notices and orders to the business owners.

- **Improvement notices** can be issued where there is a failure to comply with hygiene or food processing regulations. An example might be where there was a damaged work surface on which food was being prepared. The notice details how the regulations have not been met, describes the actions required to meet regulations, and gives a time limit for compliance. The owners can appeal against improvement notices and request that they be allowed to take alternative actions to those required by the notice.

- **Prohibition orders** are issued where the business owner has been convicted of an offence under the Food Safety Act and where a magistrate believes that there is a risk to public health. The order prevents the food business using the item, premises or process causing the risk. So if the business failed to comply with a notice requiring them to repair a work surface and the surface had deteriorated when the inspector revisited, a prohibition order might be issued. A prohibition order can also be served on an individual to ban them from running a food business for a minimum of six months. The order must be displayed prominently on the premises.

- **Emergency prohibition orders** will be issued where an officer believes there is an imminent risk of injury to health. The officer must then take the case before a magistrate within three days to confirm the order. The business owners can attend the hearing to put their case. If the court agrees with the officer, the premises or part of them must remain closed until any required work has been carried out. The order must be displayed on the premises in a conspicuous position. It will be lifted when the local authority issues a certificate to say the matter has been resolved. An emergency prohibition order might be issued where an inspector noticed infestation by cockroaches on food premises.

In addition, the Secretary of State for Health or the Minister of Agriculture, Fisheries and Food (or relevant counterparts in Scotland and Wales) can make emergency control orders. These stop the commercial operations of a food business and local environmental health officers may be required to restrict the movement of food from any business premises. One of these might be issued where the produce of a food business was considered to be unsafe.

DID YOU KNOW?

Emergency control orders are rarely issued. In 1998, Public Health Minister Tessa Jowell signed the first ever order issued under the 1990 Act. It was issued to prevent the sale of cheese from a cheese producer whose product appeared to be contaminated with *E. coli*. It was lifted after tests had been carried out and the suspected sources of the contamination had been addressed.

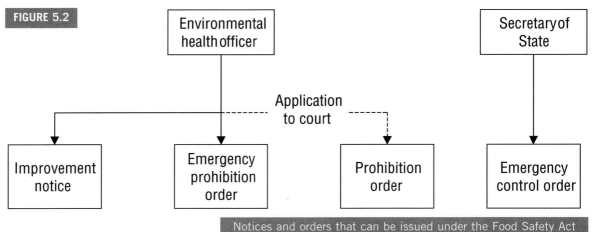

Notices and orders that can be issued under the Food Safety Act

PENALTIES

Courts have the power to impose the following penalties on business owners if they are convicted of an offence:

■ Fines up to £5000 and/or up to three months in prison. This is for minor offences, such as obstructing officers in the course of their duty.

■ Unlimited fines and/or up to two years in prison. This is used to punish serious offences that have been tried in a Crown Court, for example selling food which is harmful to health.

The court can also require the business to make a payment for compensation to anyone who has been injured by their actions.

Business owners can offer a defence in court. They need to show that they did take all reasonable steps to avoid committing any offence and to prevent any employees committing an offence. This is known as a defence of 'due diligence'. A successful defence will probably show that the business has a proper control system covering all requirements of the legislation and regulations, that staff are trained in relation to the controls, and that the system is monitored and amended as appropriate.

 STUDENT ACTIVITY 23
What records should a food business keep that may help show due diligence if required in a court of law?

THE FOOD SAFETY (GENERAL FOOD HYGIENE) REGULATIONS 1995

The main regulations made under the Food Safety Act are The Food Safety (General Food Hygiene) Regulations 1995. They incorporate the rules set out in the European Food Hygiene Directive which are applied in all EU countries. The regulations apply to anyone who handles food or works with articles that come into contact with food, such as refrigeration engineers and contract cleaners.

Owners of food businesses must ensure that operations are carried out hygienically, that all food handlers are trained and that every step is taken to ensure food safety. Operations include all stages of food preparation, distribution and sale.

The main provisions are summarised below.

Premises, vehicles and equipment

Premises, vehicles and equipment should:

■ be of a suitable design for easy cleaning

■ be in good working order

■ be properly cleaned on a regular basis

■ protect food against contamination

■ be adequately lit

■ be properly ventilated

■ have suitable drainage and an adequate water supply.

In addition, surfaces in food preparation areas should be properly maintained and easy to clean. Separate facilities must be provided for washing and disinfecting tools and equipment, and washing food.

Facilities for waste

Waste storage and disposal must be adequate. Waste should be stored in closed containers, removed from food-handling areas as soon as possible and regularly removed from the premises. Refuse areas should be kept clean and tidy.

Vehicles for transporting food

Vehicles for transporting food should be specifically designed for the purpose and kept clean. Where appropriate, they should be refrigerated. Different products should be separated in the vehicle to prevent contamination.

Washing and sanitary facilities

Washing and sanitary facilities should be adequate for staff. Changing facilities should be provided where necessary. Hand-washing facilities must be separate from those for washing food and have hot and cold running water. Suitable soap and hand-drying facilities must be provided. Lavatories must not lead directly into food rooms.

Food handlers

Food handlers should wear suitable protective clothing and maintain high standards of personal hygiene. Staff suffering illness or infection should not be allowed to handle food. Staff should be trained to a level appropriate to their work activities and should be properly supervised.

Food hazards

Food hazards must be identified, controlled and monitored, for example by use of HACCP (see Chapter 4).

Under the regulations, environmental health officers have a duty to minimise risks to public health and stop any breaches of regulations. They must carry out regular inspections of premises. They should assess any risks with regard to the nature of the food and the way it is handled, packaged, processed, displayed and stored. Any

adverse findings should be reported to the proprietor informally before any issue of a formal improvement notice.

THE FOOD PREMISES (REGISTRATION) REGULATIONS 1991

Food premises should be registered with local authorities. This includes the registration of vehicles and movable premises but excludes some businesses such as childminding that operate from domestic premises.

THE FOOD SAFETY (TEMPERATURE CONTROL) REGULATIONS 1995

Generally, all foods must be held at a temperature that will prevent the growth of pathogenic bacteria. While the regulations specify some maximum and minimum temperatures, it is implied that if specific foods are likely to become unsafe at these temperatures, then they should be held at more appropriate temperatures.

The regulations cover chilling, hot holding and cooling:

- Chilling – 8°C is the maximum temperature except where specific foods would become unsafe at this temperatures. Food for service or display can be kept out of chill temperatures for up to four hours.
- Hot holding – food must be kept at 63°C or above except where a lower temperature can be shown not to harm specific foods.
- Cooling – food that requires cooling must be cooled as quickly as possible and then kept at chill temperatures.

The DoH produces guidance notes on temperatures which are available to food businesses. (Note that the regulations are slightly different in Scotland and Scottish local authorities should be contacted for details.)

THE FOOD LABELLING REGULATIONS 1996

The principal provisions of the regulations are to require most food which is ready for delivery to the consumer or to a catering establishment to be labelled with:

- the name of the food
- a list of ingredients
- best before/use by dates
- any special storage conditions or conditions of use
- the name and address of the manufacturer or packer or seller
- an indication of the minimum or maximum percentage of an ingredient where the labelling of a food places special emphasis on the presence or low content of that ingredient.

Some food labels will also need to show:

- particulars of the place of origin of the food
- instructions for use.

The regulations prohibit the labelling or advertising of a food to claim that it has tonic or medicinal properties, and imposes conditions for certain claims relating to foods, for example reduced or low energy value claims, vitamin and mineral claims and cholesterol claims. Some labelling regulations relate to specific foods.

FIGURE 5.3

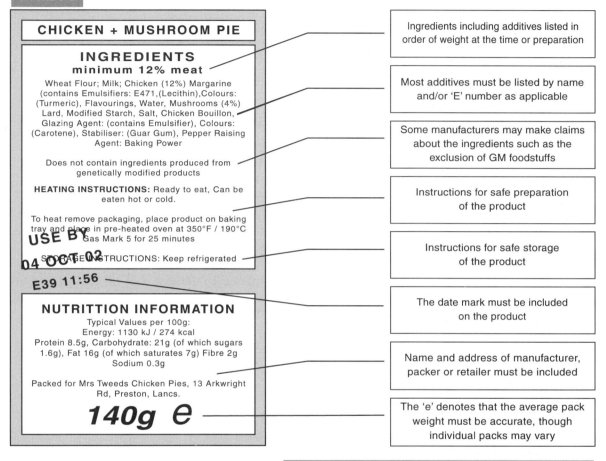

Food labels need to show a large amount of information

THE FRESH MEAT (HYGIENE AND INSPECTION) REGULATIONS 1995

- Fresh meat covers meat from cattle, pigs, sheep, goats, horses and farmed game mammals but not rabbits. The regulations also cover chilled and frozen meat.
- Premises that come under the regulations are slaughterhouses, cutting premises and cold stores. Premises for these purposes have to be approved and will be supervised by official veterinary surgeons and meat inspectors employed by the Meat Hygiene Service.

- Vets must ensure that the production of meat is hygienic and can examine carcasses and take samples. They can prohibit the slaughter of dirty animals.

- Any meat passed for human consumption is given a health mark which shows the licence number of the premises.

- Fresh meat cannot be sold for human consumption unless it has been slaughtered in licensed premises, bears the health mark showing it is fit for human consumption and, where it is transported, carries appropriate documentation.

The following regulations make similar provisions in relation to other fresh meats:

- The Poultry Meat, Farmed Game Bird Meat and Rabbit Meat (Hygiene and Inspection) Regulations 1995

- The Wild Game Meat (Hygiene and Inspection) Regulations 1995.

THE MEAT PRODUCTS (HYGIENE) REGULATIONS 1994

- Meat products covered are those where the meat has undergone treatment from heat or other means so that it no longer has the appearance of fresh meat. Examples are bacon, ham, cooked meats and meat pies.

- Premises are those producing meat products and are classified by local authorities as industrial (production in excess of 7.5 tonnes per week) and non-industrial. Non-industrial premises are relieved from some regulatory requirements. (The regulations do not apply to establishments which sell direct to consumers, such as butchers and bakers.)

- Operators of production establishments are required to ensure that critical points are identified, controlled and monitored, any samples are sent to approved laboratories, health marks are applied correctly, staff are properly trained, any products presenting a health risk are removed from sale.

THE MINCED MEAT AND MEAT PREPARATIONS (HYGIENE) REGULATIONS 1995

- This includes meat that has undergone treatment or contains additives which alter it from its fresh meat state. An example is sausage meat.

- Premises are those producing minced meat and meat preparations and are classified by local authorities as industrial (those that produce mince and those which produce in excess of 7.5 tonnes per week) and non-industrial. Non-industrial premises are relieved from some regulatory requirements. (The regulations do not apply to establishments which sell direct to consumers such as butchers and bakers.)

- Compliance requirements are similar to those for meat products (above) with the added criteria that the mince and meat preparations comply with given micro-biological limits and that recommended storage temperatures and use by dates are shown clearly on the packaging.

THE DAIRY PRODUCTS (HYGIENE) REGULATIONS 1995 (AS AMENDED 1996)

- Regulations cover all milk production on farms (from any milk-producing animals) and give microbiological standards for raw milk, treated milk, cream, ice cream and cheese.
- Farms producing milk must be registered with the Ministry for Agriculture, Fisheries and Food.
- Premises where milk is processed or handled must be approved by the Food Authority. To gain approval, they must meet hygiene standards. They will then be given a health mark which must be used on products.
- Raw milk and raw milk products must be labelled as such and are specially controlled.
- Other controls include those over storage temperatures, labelling and hazard analysis.

Required standards for skimmed, semi-skimmed and whole milk are contained in the *Drinking Milk Regulations 1976*.

THE ICE CREAM (HEAT TREATMENT) REGULATIONS 1959 (AS AMENDED)

These give standards for treatment of ice cream made from vegetable fat and storage temperatures for ice cream.

THE EGG PRODUCT REGULATIONS 1993 (AS AMENDED)

- Premises used for heat treatments of egg products should be approved by the Food Authority, and will need to comply with hygiene requirements in order to use a health mark.
- All egg products must bear a health mark.
- The regulations provide standards for pasteurisation and microbiology, as well as specifying storage temperatures.
- Egg products can only use eggs where the membrane (beneath the shell) is not damaged.

Owing to the problems with *Salmonella* and eggs, the Government recommended that eggs were not eaten in their raw state, and that vulnerable groups (children, elderly, the sick and pregnant women) should avoid dishes where the eggs are not cooked through.

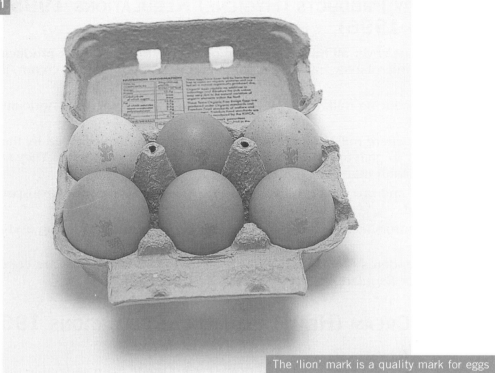

The 'lion' mark is a quality mark for eggs

CONTROL OF SUBSTANCES HAZARDOUS TO HEALTH REGULATIONS 1994 (COSHH)

FIGURE 5.4

Corrosive

Toxic

Explosive

Harmful or irritant

Flammable

All chemicals will show a hazard warning

Although not specifically concerned with food, the COSHH regulations are important in relation to chemicals used for cleaning purposes on food premises. Employers have a legal responsibility to assess the risks to employees from hazardous substances. Employees must be provided with appropriate protection and training as well as being instructed as to actions required in case of accident. Chemicals will be labelled by manufacturers as toxic, irritant, corrosive or harmful. Any warnings and instructions for use should always be noted.

The Food Standards Act 1999

The main purpose of The Food Standards Act was to set up the Food Standards Agency. This agency is an independent watchdog for food safety, with powers to protect the public health in relation to food. The Agency came into existence in April 2000. It has a similar role to the Health and Safety Executive and Commission which controls occupational health and safety standards. Responsibilities include:

- developing policies relating to matters connected with food safety or other interests of consumers in relation to food
- providing advice, information or assistance in relation to food safety to any public authority
- obtaining, compiling and reviewing information about food safety and other interests of consumers in relation to food such as monitoring and researching developments in food science and technology
- monitoring the enforcement of food safety and related legislation including setting standards of performance for enforcement.

The agency has set itself aims to reduce incidences of food-related illness and improve knowledge and practice of food hygiene across the whole population.

New laws and regulations are issued all the time to regulate different areas of the food industry. Food handlers should always be aware of legislation in the area in which they work and have a responsibility to keep up to date. For recent legislation, check the Government Stationery Office (HMSO) website or the website of the Food Standards Agency (see Appendix 1).

Summary of legal responsibilities

It is useful to summarise the legal responsibilities of managers and food handlers.

MANAGER'S RESPONSIBILITIES

It is the legal responsibility of management in any business where food is prepared and/or served to identify the specific hazards within their business and take action to minimise or control them.

Management should:

- identify food safety hazards in the workplace

- recognise how these hazards can be minimised
- implement procedures to deal with hazards
- review controls regularly and correct any problems.

FOOD HANDLER'S RESPONSIBILITIES

It is the responsibility of food handlers to:

- follow all food safety rules laid down by the employer
- protect food from contamination
- report any potential hazards or other problems to managers.

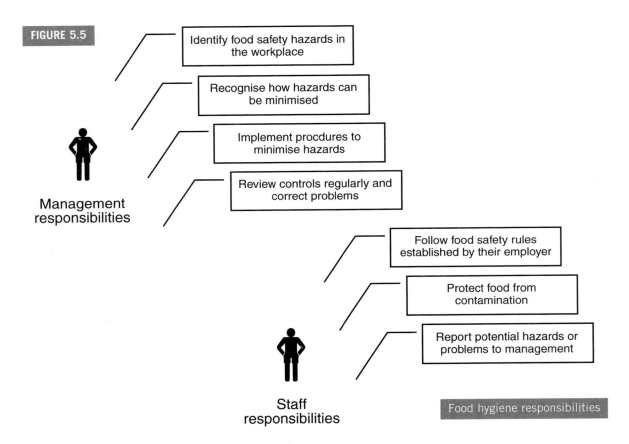

FIGURE 5.5

Identify food safety hazards in the workplace

Recognise how hazards can be minimised

Implement procdures to minimise hazards

Review controls regularly and correct problems

Management responsibilities

Follow food safety rules established by their employer

Protect food from contamination

Report potential hazards or problems to management

Staff responsibilities

Food hygiene responsibilities

Chapter review

This chapter has given you a short introduction to the main food hygiene legislation. It has also made you aware of some of the offences that can be committed by those involved in food-handling businesses and the penalties they may face.

Multiple-choice questions

1   Which of the following is an offence under the Food Safety Act 1990?
   A   Selling food that is not properly weighed
   B   Selling food that is not properly wrapped
   C   Selling food that is not contaminated
   D   Selling food which is not of the quality demanded by the purchaser

2   Which of the following reflects possible penalties for a minor offence under food safety legislation?
   A   Fines up to £2000
   B   Imprisonment up to six months
   C   Either of the above
   D   Fines up to £5000 and/or three months' imprisonment

3   Which of the following describes an improvement notice that might be issued under food safety legislation?
   A   A notice that prevents the business owners from trading
   B   A notice declaring the premises a danger to public health
   C   A notice identifying areas where regulations have not been met
   D   A notice that suggests general improvements to food hygiene

4   Which of the following describes where and how hand-washing should be carried out?
   A   Hands should only be washed in basins specifically supplied for that purpose
   B   Hands may only be washed in basins when washing-up has been cleared
   C   Hands should be washed only in basins provided in the toilet area
   D   Hands can be washed at any basin provided for washing food

5   What do food labels have to show?
   A   'use by' and 'best before' information
   B   'use by' or 'best before' information
   C   'display until' and 'use by' information
   D   It is up to the manufacturer

6   Which of the following is a legal responsibility of food handlers?

  A   To carry out a risk assessment

  B   To protect food from contamination

  C   Just to do as their employers tell them

  D   They have no legal responsibility, only a moral one

7   Which of the following is a power of environmental health officers in relation to food premises?

  A   Entering business premises

  B   Taking food for analysis

  C   Requiring co-operation from employees of the business

  D   All of the above

8   Which of the following reflects the purpose of the Food Standards Agency?

  A   It was set up as an independent watchdog for food safety

  B   It was set up to advise food businesses on hygiene

  C   It was set up to advise the Government on food standards

  D   It was set up to tell the public about food

9   Which of the following reflects the legal provisions relating to vehicles used for transporting food?

  A   Vehicles need to be specifically designed for carrying food and refrigerated

  B   Vehicles need to be specifically designed for carrying food and refrigerated if appropriate

  C   Any vehicle can be used provided it is refrigerated

  D   Any vehicle can be used

10   In which of the following cases is a prohibition order likely to be issued?

  A   An inspector finds cockroaches in a restaurant

  B   An inspector receives a complaint about a restaurant

  C   The manager of a food business becomes ill with food poisoning

  D   All of the above

Short-answer questions

1   Describe the basic information that is required on food labels.
2   State the hand-washing facilities which must be provided for food handlers.
3   Explain the powers of environmental health officers in relation to food premises.
4   Explain the regulations relating to fresh meat.
5   Explain the function of Government Codes of Practice.

Answers to student activities

Student activity 1

You should have identified that food poisoning or food-related illness:

- is relatively common
- that most people don't see a doctor
- that common symptoms are diarrhoea, sickness and abdominal pain.

Student activity 2

INFECTIOUS FOOD POISONING

Salmonella

TOXIN IN FOOD

Clostridium botulinum

Bacillus cereus

Staphylococcus aureus

TOXIN IN INTESTINES

Clostridium perfringens

Bacillus cereus

Student activity 3

You should have identified the following organisms:

Tony: *Salmonella*

Derbyshire Town: *E. coli*

Mary: *Listeria*.

Student activity 4

- Raw meat left at room temperature – very likely to become contaminated, provides perfect breeding ground for micro-organisms and should be kept at chill temperatures.
- Pickled onions – unlikely to grow pathogens due to high acidity level.
- Rice pudding left in a saucepan on the hob to cool down – milk and milk products are very susceptible to micro-organisms and this will provide a warm, wet, nutritious environment for them!
- Dried mushrooms – probably not enough moisture for bacteria to grow.

Student activity 5

Your answer will depend on the type of food you have chosen. Table 2.1 (reproduced below) identifies common signs of spoilage.

Table 2.1 Signs of spoilage in food

Type of food	Common signs of spoilage
Milk	Smells and tastes 'off'. Starts to curdle so bits are found in the milk
Vegetables	Become soft and discoloured. May have black spots. Smell rotten
Fish	Smells 'off' and discolours
Processed/cooked meats	Surface slime and discoloration. Smells 'off'. Produces gases that may burst vacuum packs
Fresh meats/poultry	Surface slime. Green discoloration. White spots. Smells 'off'
Bread	Fruity, sickly smell. Soft sticky texture. Internally bread discolours to yellow or brown

Student activity 6

- Cockroaches – carry pathogenic micro-organisms such as *Salmonella* and can physically contaminate food with egg cases, faeces, and dead bodies.
- Rodents – carry pathogenic and spoilage micro-organisms and can physically contaminate food with droppings, urine, fur or dead bodies. Rodents can also cause physical damage to wiring, pipes and woodwork, which causes further hazards.
- Bluebottles – carry pathogenic micro-organisms and spoilage bacteria on their bodies. Defecate and regurgitate previous meals on to food as they eat. Eggs and live or dead larvae and insects can contaminate food.

Student activity 7

Hazards include:

- rubbish overflowing
- spills on the work surface
- cat sitting on work surface
- cat's food dishes on the floor
- generally untidy and unclean
- open can not disposed of on draining area
- pie near open window attracting insects
- cakes next to washing-up water
- bleach could contaminate food
- someone's shoes left on floor
- pan left on heating element
- spider and spider's web
- knife left overhanging edge of work surface
- mouse coming out of cupboard.

Student activity 8

You may have included some or all of the following:

- removing any jewellery, hair ornaments or similar
- tying back and covering hair
- changing into appropriate clothing
- washing – at least hands.

Student activity 9

- Thawing a frozen chicken – risk that centre not properly thawed and may carry *Salmonella*. Allow time for thawing.
- Cooking a previously frozen chicken – if not properly thawed, may not be sufficiently cooked in centre to destroy micro-organisms. Allow adequate cooking times and temperatures.
- Storing seafood – seafood is a high-risk food and needs to be stored at chill temperatures to ensure micro-organisms do not grow.
- Serving food from a hot holding area – hot held food needs to be at above 63°C to ensure that micro-organisms cannot grow.

Student activity 10

Hazards are:

∎ open door
∎ spillage from bottle on top shelf
∎ open containers and unwrapped foods
∎ raw and cooked foods stored on same shelf
∎ raw food juices contaminating other foods on lower shelves
∎ untidily stacked – no organisation
∎ opened cans – contents not transferred to suitable containers.

Student activity 11

∎ Raw meat – needs to be kept at chill temperatures to prevent micro-organism growth. Should be stored separately from cooked foods to prevent cross-contamination, especially by meat juices dripping onto other food items. If stored in a refrigerator with other items should be stored on the bottom shelf.

∎ Flour – needs to be stored in a cool, dry place in lidded containers to prevent infestation by insects. Some infestations unavoidable when they come in contact with the flour.

∎ Canned foods – need to be stored so they are not damaged, and properly rotated so that earlier purchases are used first. Blown or dented cans should not be used as, if the contents have been exposed to the air, they may be contaminated by micro-organisms.

∎ Cleaning materials – need to be stored away from food, preferably in a locked cupboard under the control of a responsible person. Risks are tainting and poisoning of food if they come into contact.

Student activity 12

Obviously everyone has different tastes so your list will be different from others. There are a wide range of preserved foods that have a different taste and texture from fresh produce. You may have included the following among your likes and dislikes:

∎ pickles
∎ jams and preserves
∎ smoked fish or meats
∎ tinned fruits, vegetables, fish or meats
∎ dried fruits.

There are lots more examples.

Student activity 13

These are the main methods of preservation we have identified:

▋ drying or removing or reducing moisture

▋ pickling

▋ smoking

▋ using chemical preservatives

▋ heat treatments – sterilising or pasteurising

▋ chilling – refrigerating

▋ freezing

▋ vacuum packing

▋ irradiation.

Student activity 14

These are the processes used to control the growth of micro-organisms.

▋ Drying or removing or reducing moisture – removal of one of growth requirements – moisture

▋ Pickling – combination of removal of one of growth requirements and chemical preservatives – changes pH by addition of chemicals

▋ Smoking – combination of removal of one of growth requirements and chemical preservatives – changes pH and salts usually added which preserve the food

▋ Heat treatments – sterilising or pasteurising – destroy bacteria or reduce to lower levels and seal them out. Pasteurised products will usually require refrigeration

▋ Canning – destroys bacteria and seals them out

▋ Chilling – refrigerating – too cold for most organisms to grow – need higher temperatures

▋ Freezing – too cold for organisms to grow and moisture is turned to ice – need higher temperatures and moisture

▋ Vacuum packing – excludes oxygen which organisms need to grow

▋ Modified Atmosphere Packing – uses gases to exclude oxygen

▋ Irradiation – electrically charges the food particles which stops micro-organisms from growing

Student activity 15

- Dry storage areas – provide food, shelter, and warmth.
- Cracks and holes in fabric of building – provide shelter and nest places.
- Waste storage areas – provide food, and nest sites.

Student activity 16

Your flowchart should look something like this:

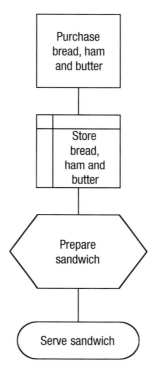

Making a ham sandwich

Student activity 17

Table A.1: The hazards of ham sandwiches

Steps in the process	Hazards What can go wrong?	Controls What can I do about it?	Monitor How can I check?
Purchase of bread, butter and ham	• Bought ingredients could be contaminated with bacteria, mould or foreign bodies • Ingredients could be contaminated during delivery • Ham and butter could be at inappropriate temperature on delivery	• Use reputable suppliers for breads, meats and dairy products • Check goods on receipt for damage	• Check delivery vehicles • Check date marks • Check temperatures • Check food condition
Store bread, butter and ham	• Contamination could take place during storage • Cross-contamination could take place during storage	• Store bread wrapped and in suitable container • Use proper stock rotation – First in, First out • Store butter on top shelf of fridge, ham on middle shelves • Keep separate from raw meat products	• Check storage temperatures • Check storage conditions
Prepare sandwich	• Contamination or cross-contamination from other foods, food handlers, utensils or equipment	• Limit handling • Good personal hygiene of food handlers • Food handlers properly trained • Surfaces and utensils clean • Use separate utensils and surfaces for cutting meat and buttering bread • Don't cut ham on surfaces or with utensils used for raw meats	• Visual checks on food areas, food handlers etc. • Cleaning schedules
Serve sandwich	• Contamination before serving	• Serving areas clean • Food served immediately or covered and stored in a cool place • Good personal hygiene of serving staff	• Visual checks of food, food areas and procedures (check food not left before serving)

Student activity 18

You should have identified some or all of the following:

- not washing hands before starting work
- not washing hands between tasks, for example touching waste, then food; touching raw foods, then cooked foods.
- not washing hands after visiting the toilet
- handling food when suffering from food-borne illness
- sneezing or coughing over food
- touching hair, face, nose or mouth before handling food
- using dirty utensils, especially those used for raw foods, on cooked foods
- not cleaning work surfaces between food preparation tasks.

Student activity 19

Hazards include:

- microbiological hazards from dirty clothes, outdoor clothes, non-protective clothing worn in food preparation areas
- physical hazards from loose fastenings or clothes in poor state of repair, hairs if not covered, items falling from pockets or person (combs, pens, jewellery, etc.).

Student activity 20

There will be a wide variety of answers, and some will cross areas, but the following are given as examples:

- production – meat, crop and dairy farms
- processing – frozen vegetable processors, canning factories, meat curing
- preparation – restaurants, establishments producing ready meals, supermarkets, bakeries and butchers who prepare ready-to-eat foods
- serving – restaurants, airlines, railways, hotels
- selling – supermarkets, greengrocers, bakeries, butchers, vending machines.

Student activity 21

Cleaning is important to prevent microbiological and physical contamination of food, to prevent pest infestation and to present the right image to customers.

Areas to be regularly cleaned include:

■ all food preparation and serving areas
■ food storage areas including dry storage, chill rooms and refrigerators
■ delivery areas
■ food display cabinets – either chill or hot cabinets
■ delivery vehicles where these are used by the business
■ sanitary, washing and changing areas
■ external areas where waste is stored.

Student activity 22

It is the responsibility of managers and supervisors to ensure that:

■ proper cleaning schedules are in place and are followed
■ proper records are kept of cleaning
■ appropriate persons are responsible for cleaning tasks
■ there are enough cleaning staff
■ cleaning is carried out safely
■ equipment is appropriate for the task, and properly cleaned and stored after use.

Student activity 23

Records should be kept of the following:

■ risk assessment and hazard controls (HACCP)
■ staff training
■ cleaning schedule and the dates and times that cleaning tasks are carried out
■ maintenance and service records for equipment
■ temperature checks on storage, display, etc.
■ stock control
■ checks made on receipt of deliveries.

Answers to multiple-choice questions

Chapter 1

1 **D** Keeping food safe at all stages of processing
2 **C** Illness caused by harmful substances or micro-organisms in the food
3 **A** Food that contains anything that is harmful to health
4 **A** They are sometimes helpful
5 **D** Micro-organisms that cause illness and disease
6 **B** Abdominal pain, diarrhoea and vomiting
7 **B** Toxic plankton
8 **C** *Clostridium perfringens*
9 **A** Vomiting, diarrhoea, abdominal pain and fever
10 **D** Eggs

Chapter 2

1 **C** Each cell splits into two
2 **B** A few hours
3 **B** Between 5 °C and 63 °C
4 **D** All of the above
5 **B** Pesticides
6 **C** They are used in some food production
7 **A** They can survive in adverse conditions
8 **C** Insect eggs
9 **B** Eggs
10 **A** Jam

Chapter 3

1 **C** It stops bacteria reproducing temporarily
2 **B** They should be cooled quickly and stored at below 8 °C
3 **A** Foods purchased first should be used first
4 **A** Cooling
5 **B** Above 63 °C
6 **D** Raw foods should be stored on a lower shelf than cooked foods
7 **C** The hot food will raise the temperature of the freezer
8 **A** −18 °C
9 **B** In lidded bins
10 **D** Cockroach eggs

Chapter 4

1 **B** To prevent food from becoming contaminated
2 **A** Because you could be a carrier of the illness without knowing
3 **B** After cleaning
4 **D** All of the above
5 **C** To identify food hazards and prevent or minimise them
6 **B** To reduce micro-organisms to a safe level
7 **C** Cleaning removes dirt and disinfecting reduces bacteria
8 **D** A wound on the hand
9 **A** Pre-clean, clean, rinse, disinfect, final rinse, dry
10 **D** So they can be seen if they fall into food

Chapter 5

1 **D** Selling food which is not of the quality demanded by the purchaser

2 **D** Fines up to £5000 and/or three months' imprisonment

3 **C** A notice identifying areas where regulations have not been met

4 **A** Hands should only be washed in basins specifically supplied for that purpose

5 **B** 'use by' dates or 'best before' information

6 **B** To protect food from contamination

7 **D** All of the above

8 **A** It was set up as an independent watchdog for food safety

9 **B** Vehicles need to be specifically designed for carrying food and refrigerated if appropriate

10 **A** An inspector finds cockroaches in a restaurant

Appendix:
Useful websites

As food hygiene and safety knowledge and regulations are constantly changing, the most useful resources are those on the Internet, which are updated regularly. The following are useful websites for information about food hygiene issues:

Chartered Institute of Environmental Health	www.cieh.org.uk
Department of Health	www.doh.gov.uk
Food Standards Agency	www.food.gov.uk
Her Majesty's Stationery Office	www.hmso.gov.uk
Public Health Laboratory Service	www.phls.org.uk
Royal Institute of Public Health	www.riph.org.uk

Glossary

Cleaning the process of removing dirt

Contamination
when unwanted items or bacteria are present in food

Cross-contamination
when micro-organisms are moved from one place to another on a vehicle

Disinfection
destruction of micro-organisms to a level not hazardous to health or likely to cause food spoilage

FIFO stock rotation
first in, first out. Foods that were obtained first should be used first

Food anything intended for human consumption or used as an ingredient in the preparation of food

Hazard anything that could potentially cause harm. Generally divided into biological, physical or chemical hazards

High-risk foods
these include those that are high in protein and moist, such as meat, fish, shellfish, poultry, eggs, milk and dairy products, cooked rice and pasta

Host organism
the person, animal or plant infected with the micro-organism

Incubation period
the length of time normally taken for symptoms of the illness to appear

Micro-organisms
very small life forms such as bacteria and viruses

Multi-cellular
consisting of more than one cell

Pathogenic micro-organisms or pathogens
micro-organisms that cause illnesses

Risk the likelihood that a hazard will occur

Spoilage the process of food becoming damaged. Spoilage bacteria will make food rot

Spore a hard, resistant body formed within the bacterial cell

Toxins poisons produced by some bacteria and moulds

Vehicle of contamination
any object (including persons and animals) on which micro-organisms can move from one place to another

Index